The Socioeconomic Impact of Pandemics

Orhan Erdem

The Socioeconomic Impact of Pandemics

How COVID-19 Reshaped the World

palgrave
macmillan

Orhan Erdem
University of North Texas
Denton, TX, USA

ISBN 978-3-032-24188-7 ISBN 978-3-032-24189-4 (eBook)
https://doi.org/10.1007/978-3-032-24189-4

This Palgrave Macmillan imprint is published by the registered company Springer Nature Switzerland AG.
The registered company address is: Gewerbestrasse 11, 6330 Cham, Switzerland

For Şükran, Osman, and Ömer

"A terrific book that weaves history, literature, and modern analysis into a clear and compelling narrative. Drawing on voices from Camus, Vonnegut, and Marcus Aurelius, alongside vivid storytelling such as the Dr. Karikó case, it makes sense of one of the most disorienting crises of our time without losing nuance or humanity. Above all, it captures the central truths of crisis: that the vulnerable suffer most; fear erodes logic; and democracy itself is at risk. A thoughtful, heterodox work with a final line that lingers long after the last page."

—Robert Maranto, *University of Arkansas*

"In a literature overflowing with narrow studies, Erdem offers something rare: a panoramic, rigorously researched, and deeply humane account of how COVID-19 reshaped economies, politics, education, and daily life. Essential reading for scholars, policymakers, and anyone seeking to understand what the pandemic truly cost us."

—Isa Hafalir, Professor of Economics, *University of Technology Sydney*

Acknowledgments

I am deeply grateful to Robert Maranto, Mehmet Dik, Denise Philpot, and Mehmet Berksan, who read the manuscript in its entirety with exceptional care and patience. Their detailed, thoughtful feedback sharpened arguments, exposed blind spots, and improved the clarity of the work. This book is stronger because of their careful attention and intellectual generosity.

Competing Interests The author has no competing interests to declare that are relevant to the content of this manuscript.

Contents

List of Figures

List of Tables

PART I

Introduction

CHAPTER 1

From Apollo's Arrow to COVID-19

Abstract This chapter places COVID-19 within a broader historical context, showing that pandemics are not rare exceptions but recurring events that have repeatedly reshaped societies. Drawing on examples such as the Plague of Athens, it illustrates how crises tend to hit the most vulnerable the hardest. More importantly, it argues that the consequences of a pandemic are determined not only by the disease itself, but also by how societies choose to respond to it. The chapter sets up the book's main argument: while many COVID-19 policies helped reduce health risks, they also created substantial long-term economic and social costs that need careful assessment.

Keywords Pandemics • COVID-19 • Inequality • Medical history • Crisis response • Scientific progress • Public health • Policy trade-offs

Outbreaks are inevitable, but pandemics are optional.
—Dr. Larry Brilliant, 2015

The history of humanity is full of crises. Every crisis, whether a plague, pandemic, financial, or economic, substantially reshapes the way we live. In recent decades, disease-driven crises have become increasingly common.[1] Yet, time and again, it is the disadvantaged, the poor and the vulnerable who suffer most.

O. Erdem, *The Socioeconomic Impact of Pandemics*,
https://doi.org/10.1007/978-3-032-24189-4_1

This book is about one such crisis: The COVID-19 pandemic. Yet COVID-19 is not the first epidemic to reshape societies, and challenge humans. To understand what was uniquie about COVID, it is useful to place it within a much longer history of disease outbreaks and the lessons they left behind.

The Plague of Athens erupted during the second year of the Peloponnesian War, around 430–426 BC, when Athens and Sparta were locked in a conflict. The epidemic spread rapidly and quickly swept through the Athenian army. It is estimated to have killed nearly 100,000 people, roughly 25% of the population. The epidemic crippled Athens in both military and political terms, even claiming the life of the prominent Athenian general Pericles. The people of the city-state started to believe that it was Apollo, the god of oracles, music, disease, and medicine, who had sent the plague to Greece with one of his arrows. Hence the name later given to the plague: Apollo's arrow.

Greek Athenian historian Thucydides, who also contracted the disease and recovered, wrote that it took 15 years for the Athenian population to recover. In truth, Athens never fully regained its former strength. The plague marked the beginning of a long decline in its power and prestige.[2]

Later, the Antonine Plague, named after Marcus Aurelius Antonius, erupted around 165 AD during the reign of emperor and philosopher Marcus Aurelius and marked the first of many empire-wide pandemics in Roman history. It is believed that the disease entered the empire from the Roman soldiers returning from wars in the East. As the disease spread across the empire's vast cities, it killed both civilians and soldiers alike. Historians estimate that the pandemic claimed between 60 and 70 million lives, amounting to roughly a quarter to a third of the population at the time.[3] It struck deep into the empire's urban centers and frontier regions, from Egypt to Gaul, Syria to the Danube. This immense loss of life weakened the Roman Empire and made it vulnerable during the Marcomannic Wars (166–180 AD). The plague had a serious impact on the economy. In places like Egypt, the silver coins were made with less silver (debasement of money). Prices of goods rose quickly, and the value of the money dropped by half. Land prices dropped sharply, likely because people no longer needed as much farmland. Farmers ended up paying much less to rent land, and this lower cost remained for decades.[4] Marcus Aurelius battled not only wars but also the plague, ultimately dying from the disease on March 17, 180 AD.[5] Some thought it was the god Apollo again, punishing the empire. Some orators even said, "Happy they who perished in the plague!" However, the famous medical doctor of the time, Galen, said it was just a plague.[6] According to the historian and University of Oklahoma professor Kyle Harper, the pandemic started a new era in the Roman Empire.[7]

A few centuries after the Antonine Plague, the Justinian Plague emerged in an Egyptian port in 541 AD, spreading rapidly. By spring 542, it reached Constantinople, currently Istanbul, Türkiye, before sweeping through Syria, Greece, Italy, North Africa, and even reaching Ireland by 544.[8] It is interesting to note that this plague also happened after a series of Hun campaigns to Europe in the fifth century, meaning that the plague may have been carried by armies and traders. It is estimated that, at its height, it was killing around 10,000 people per day, which equates to millions of lives today. Emperor Justinian I of the Byzantine Empire, the ruler after whom the plague was named, also caught the deadly disease. Although he fell gravely ill, he ultimately survived.

The economic aftershocks of the Justinian Plague were dramatic. Because the population fell much faster than output, survivors found themselves in a world where labor was scarce and land abundant. Economic historians Şevket Pamuk and Maya Shatzmiller argue that at this time wages for unskilled workers in Egypt and Iraq rose dramatically, and prices of basic grains fell relative to manufactured goods. These shifts in relative prices, purchasing power, and labor scarcity helped weaken the old Byzantine fiscal system, leading to a reshaping of trade patterns. According to Pamuk and Shatzmiller, this weakening made the early Islamic conquests unusually easy and fast. When Islamic armies arrived in the mid-seventh century, they encountered provinces that were depopulated, demoralized, and fiscally exhausted. As a result, the Justinian Plague provided a powerful macroeconomic shock, redistributing income toward labor and helping set the stage for the early Islamic Golden Age.[9]

Even in the twentieth century, the 1918 Spanish flu, though it is far less remembered than World War I, claimed more lives than the war itself. It is estimated that between 50 to 100 million people died worldwide because of the Spanish flu, far surpassing the roughly 10 to 20 million lives lost in World War I.[10] During the Spanish flu, societies struggled not only with the virus itself but also with superstition and misinformation (both by the public and the government). These patterns echo across the centuries: it is our beliefs, fears, and responses that often shape the trajectory of a pandemic as much as the virus.

A couple of important observations might be worth noting with regard to the history of major plagues.

First, some of the big plagues have changed the history of humanity in profound ways. The effects of the Spanish flu, for example, remained visible well into the 1980s. Individuals who were in utero during the pandemic completed less schooling, had lower socioeconomic status, and experienced higher disability rates. The 1919 birth cohort's reduced education and earnings alone are estimated to be more than $14 billion in lifetime economic losses.[11] Similarly, when Europeans arrived in the Americas after 1492, they carried pathogens that spread faster than their armies. It is estimated that roughly 95% of Native American deaths across the Americas were caused by introduced diseases rather than by warfare.[12] In the Inca Empire, the first wave of smallpox alone is believed to have killed nearly half the population.

Second, these plagues claimed millions of lives and often recurred in repeated waves. Hence, we continue to be surprised by their emergence. Third, pandemics have always been associated with godly wrath, superstition, and false beliefs.

Between 2020 and 2022, the world faced the most devastating pandemic of the century. COVID-19, caused by the SARS-CoV-2 virus, spread across the globe at an incredibly fast pace, disrupting societies, economies, and daily life. The pandemic infected over 750 million people globally and claimed more than 7 million lives, with approximately 1 million deaths occurring in the United States alone. These staggering numbers, while deeply sobering, represent only one dimension of the crisis. Beyond the immediate toll on human lives, the pandemic exposed weaknesses in healthcare systems, economies, education, supply chains, and global preparedness for such catastrophes.

In response to the crisis, an extraordinary amount of research was conducted to better understand the virus, its behavior, and the impacts of mitigation measures. Governments, scientists, and institutions worked together to document and analyze the pandemic in real time. As of the end of 2025, WorldCat, the world's largest library database, lists over 2.2 million articles and 87,000 print books, and 160,000 eBooks containing the word "COVID-19." This explosion of knowledge reflects an enormous effort to comprehend the virus, manage its spread, and mitigate its consequences. Yet, despite the breadth of this research, much of it is fragmented or confined within one discipline. Studies often answered specific questions but left the larger picture blurry. In other words, we produced a vast archive of information, but very few coherent maps. The challenge now is to make sense of this flood of knowledge, connecting historical patterns, scientific insights, and social consequences, to understand what actually happened and what it means for the future, leaving room for dissenting voices as well.

While COVID-19 may feel like it will never happen again, recent research evaluating global epidemics from 1600 to the present paints a more sobering picture. Estimates suggest the annual probability of encountering a pandemic of similar magnitude is approximately 1%. This means that over an 80-year lifespan, the chance of experiencing a similar pandemic could be as high as 54%, almost a coin flip.[13] In other words, there is an almost even chance that we will experience another pandemic of this scale within our lifetimes. This probability is a wake-up call: pandemics are not rare anomalies, but recurring events throughout history, driven by factors like globalization, urbanization, and increasing human interaction with wildlife. Every year, researchers identify between two and five zoonotic viruses, organisms such as a virus or bacterium that originate in animals and have the potential to infect humans.[14]

This realization leads us to a critical question: What happens if it happens again? The philosopher Hegel once remarked that the only thing we learn from history is that we learn nothing from history. Is this really true? Are we able to learn from COVID? Are we prepared for the next pandemic, or will history repeat itself? The measures taken during COVID-19, including lockdowns, social distancing, and the rapid development of vaccines, were unprecedented, but they sparked debates and raised questions that remain unresolved. Should we impose lockdowns again, knowing the toll they take on mental health, politics, economies, and education? How do we balance individual freedoms with collective safety in future crises?

These are not just hypothetical questions. They are urgent considerations that demand thoughtful reflection and preparation. The lessons learned from COVID-19 must inform our future responses, ensuring that when, not if, the next pandemic arrives, humanity is better equipped to minimize its impact.

This book sets the stage for exploring these questions and bridging the gap between the vast body of research on pandemics and the public's understanding of how to respond effectively, while also paying close attention to the dissenting views around pandemic policies.

As I was exploring the consequences of the pandemic in order to write this book, I realized two things: First, the burdens of the pandemic fell most heavily on the already disadvantaged, in terms of both individuals and nations. Second, many of the precautions, though well-intentioned, overshot their purpose. The social and economic costs of these measures far exceed their benefits. At both national and international levels, poverty and inequality have deepened. Similarly, global education systems were disrupted, meaning that some children will never recover the learning they lost.

Thus, I argue in this book that while the policies implemented during the COVID-19 pandemic might have saved many lives and prevented countless infections, they also came at substantial cost. This is not to suggest that such measures should never be implemented. Rather, they should be applied with careful sensitivity to their wider consequences. We should have aimed to prevent extreme costs to society and to future generations.

It is entirely possible, for example, that we would have arrived at similar health outcomes, even if schools had reopened earlier. The same caution applies to other non-pharmaceutical interventions (NPIs). Should such measures be limited, or should they be pursued whatever the cost? Many countries preferred to adopt the "whatever-it-takes" approach. Now, almost five years after the pandemic, we are finally in a position to assess how effective those choices truly were.

History suggests that societies are shaped not only by the viruses they face but also by the choices they make in response. Somewhere between hesitation and overreach lies a narrow area where the least damage is done and the greatest benefit is achieved. In the chapters that follow, I develop an idea shaped by this observation—a principle I call optimal stringency. You will explore its full shape with reasoning in each chapter.

This book, which is a culmination of my 4–5 years of effort to understand the pandemic, provides a social science perspective to the discussions. By drawing on literature, history, science, and real-world experiences, it seeks to uncover the lessons of COVID-19 and to chart a clearer path for how we might confront future pandemics with greater wisdom and balance.

Notes

1. Yong (2018)
2. Martínez (2017)
3. https://www.worldhistory.org/Antonine_Plague/
4. Harper (2017)

5. Vlach (2020)
6. Harper (2017)
7. Harper (2017, p. 81)
8. Sarris (2022)
9. Pamuk and Shatzmiller (2014)
10. Taubenberger and Morens (2006)
11. Almond (2006)
12. Diamond (2017, p. 78) and Lovgren (2005)
13. Marani et al. (2021) estimate the annual probability of a similar pandemic to be between 1/209 and 3/209. Using the average value of 2/209 as a reasonable estimate, the probability of experiencing a pandemic of this intensity over an 80-year period is calculated as: $1-\left(1-\frac{2}{209}\right)^{80}=0.54$. This corresponds to a 54% chance over a typical lifetime.
14. Hook (2020).

PART II

Then and Now

CHAPTER 2

Pale Horse

Abstract This chapter uses historical narratives and literary storytelling to explore the human experience of pandemics, drawing parallels between past outbreaks and COVID-19. By examining emotional, social, and behavioral responses to disease, it illustrates how fear, uncertainty, and denial recur across time. The chapter emphasizes that despite advances in medicine, the psychological and societal patterns of pandemics remain strikingly consistent, reinforcing the idea that history provides critical insight into modern crises.

Keywords Spanish flu • Narrative analysis • Pandemic psychology • Healthcare collapse • Trauma

Humanity has but 3 great enemies: Fever, famine, war;of these by far the greatest, by far the most terrible, is fever.

—*William Osler,* "The Study of the Fevers of the South," *1896*

Miranda, a reporter at Blue Mountain News, a local newspaper, was not aware of the impending nightmare she was about to face. Despite feeling unwell, she didn't let it disrupt her daily routine, especially enjoying her new

O. Erdem, *The Socioeconomic Impact of Pandemics*,
https://doi.org/10.1007/978-3-032-24189-4_2

romance with Adam, an Army lieutenant she met just 10 days ago. She continued embracing each day with enthusiasm, finding joy in the small moments they shared. Adam ensured to dedicate his leave time to sharing with Miranda, exploring museums, climbing mountains, attending theater plays, and dancing.

Miranda ignored her initial discomfort that day, thinking it was fatigue. However, as time went by, she suspected that her symptoms were related to the new disease, the flu pandemic, which "knocks everybody into a cocked hat." She started to feel rotten, leaving her more and more defeated.

She first fell unconscious in a restaurant while joyfully dancing with Adam. They took her to bed where she slept for hours. When she woke up, she realized that her situation was more serious than she initially thought and required hospitalization. However, hospitals were overwhelmed with critical patients, and the ambulances were in high demand. Adam, who was nursing her, called the hospital many times for an ambulance but failed to get one. It was almost impossible to find an ambulance. The city's emergency system was barely functioning, with resources depleted and personnel in short supply. Many paramedics were themselves out sick.

Things got worse. Realizing that Miranda had contracted the flu, her landlady, Miss Hobbe, threatened her with eviction unless she went to the hospital. The nightmare was growing. Miranda felt hopeless, and Adam was desperate. All Adam could do was sit beside her, talking and boosting her morale. He repeatedly kissed her on the cheek, apparently taking a risk of getting infected.

The plague and the sense of death infiltrated the entire city. Funerals crowded the streets. "All the theaters and nearly all the shops and restaurants are closed, and the streets have been full of funerals all day and ambulances all night," Adam told Miranda.

As the days passed, Miranda's condition worsened; she lost her sense of smell and hearing, and her mind started tottering. She became afraid to sleep, thinking that she might not wake up again. She was terrified of dying. She asked Adam if he could teach her a prayer, but he knew none. Instead, Miranda started whispering the words of a spiritual: "Pale horse, pale rider, done taken my lover away," referencing Revelation 6:8.

On a day when Adam was on duty, a police ambulance arrived to pick up Miranda. One of the interns carried her to the ambulance on his shoulders, as she was too weak to walk. Lightheadedly murmuring Adam's name, she felt a hope that she might have a chance to survive. She even began dreaming about her future, imagining writing more articles, having a great time with Adam, and maybe even getting married. Who knows…?

Upon arrival at the hospital, she saw a scene of despair: people crying in pain or lying speechless and motionless on the iron beds, some of them dead. Even being in the hospital did not prevent her from having scary dreams of death. She

> *was smelling death in her body. As the days went by, and her condition failed to improve, a heavy sense of hopelessness settled over the room. At some point, even doctors gave up on her. She had the sensation that the doctors, nurses, and the whole society was pushing her back onto her feet only to send her down the same path toward death. She spent some of her days in a state of unconsciousness. Sometimes, she woke up, unrecognizing her own face in the mirror. Little by little, though, that strangeness began to lift, and as the days passed, her pains gradually eased.*
>
> *One day, she awoke to voices around her bed, celebrating the Armistice; World War I was over. The nurses told her that day she was ready to leave, having recovered her health. "How come?" she thought. Her mind started thinking about what to wear, where to go, and how to see Adam again. While the cab was waiting for her at the front door, she looked at the heap of unopened letters on her desk. One was from Adam's military camp. She immediately opened it but did not recognize the handwriting. As she read the lines, she learned that Adam had died from influenza. She silently murmured, "I love you, Adam."*

This short story, *Pale Horse Pale Rider*, was written by Katherine Anne Porter and published in 1938 when she was working as a reporter at the *Rocky Mountain News* in Denver, Colorado, and the quotes belong to her.[1] *Pale Horse Pale Rider* is often regarded as one of the most accurate descriptions of the 1918 Spanish flu, and "most effective and most appropriate form of memory available to remember the pandemic."[2] It is, in fact, an autobiographical novella that testifies to Porter's traumatic memory. Porter had fallen in love with a young Army officer, Alexander Barclay, around the time she contracted influenza in 1918. Hospitalized with a 105 °F fever, her days in the hospital were horrific. She once fell and broke her elbow; another time, she developed phlebitis in her leg.[3] Her doctors believed she was nearing death, the newspaper she worked for prepared her obituary, and her family was making funeral arrangements. But she survived, mainly because of an experimental injection of strychnine.[4] Tragically, Barclay died, as depicted in the novella. The hospital stay had a profound impact on Porter's life. When she left the hospital at the age of 27, her hair had turned completely white. She described the effect of the disease on her life as follows:

> *It simply divided my life, cut across it like that... It took me a long time to go out and live in the world again. I was really 'alienated,' in the pure sense. It was, I think, the fact that I really had participated in death, that I knew what death was, and had almost experienced it. I had what the Christians call the*

'beatific vision,' and the Greeks called the 'happy day,' the happy vision just before death. Now, if you have had that, and survived it, come back from it, you are no longer like other people, and there's no use deceiving yourself that you are.[5]

After publishing this novella, which was inspired by her traumatic memory, Porter received various accolades. She has since been esteemed as one of the greatest writers of the century, having received many awards, including a Creative Arts Award for lifetime achievement, a National Book Award, and a Pulitzer Prize.[6]

World War I came to an end on November 11, 1918, when Germany was forced to sign an armistice agreement with the Allies. The war left 10 million to 20 million people dead, and many more physically scars, with much social, psychological, and mental damage in its wake. However, nobody was aware that worse was yet to come.

This was a pandemic, which was arguably the deadliest in history.

The origins of the so-called "Spanish flu," as it is generally called, remain uncertain, with theories about the location ranging from Western Europe to the U.S., even to China. The timing of its outbreak is more certain: around the spring of 1918. Given that most military battles took place on European fronts, it seems plausible to believe that the flu originated there. Whatever the origin, it is clear that it started in the spring of 1918 (Fig. 2.1).

The Spanish Flu pandemic, occurring in three waves before the Armistice, claimed the lives of 50 million people or 2.6% of the world's population at that time. Some historians estimate the death toll as high as 100 million.[7] Nonetheless, the Spanish Flu was at least five times deadlier than World War I and is often referred to as a "forgotten pandemic" or a "forgotten apocalypse." This is mainly because the mere existence of the Spanish Flu is largely ignored or overlooked, with very limited resources giving details on what happened. According to WorldCat, the world's largest library database, as of 2019 (before COVID-19), there were approximately 114,000 printed books on "First World War," 135,000 on "World War I" but only 790 printed books on "Spanish flu." Therefore, *Pale Horse, Pale Rider* stands as one of the few books on and a vivid record of the 1918 pandemic.

The "Spanish flu" was first perceived to be caused by a bacterium, called Pfeiffer's bacillus or *Haemophilus influenzae*, named after Richard Pfeiffer, a German bacteriologist who proposed a theory about the cause of influenza in 1892. Almost all physicians agreed on this, except for a few

Fig. 2.1 Edvard Munch, *Self-Portrait with the Spanish flu*, 1919. Painted shortly after recovering from the Spanish flu, Munch—best known for his iconic work *The Scream*—depicts himself weakened, seated in a wicker chair, his expression hollow and fatigued. The loose brushwork and somber palette evoke the lingering physical toll of illness and his psychological vulnerability. (Source: https://commons.wikimedia.org/wiki/File:Edvard_Munch_-_Self-Portrait_with_the_Spanish_flu_(1919).jpg)

doubters, including J. W. Nuzman of Cook County Hospital in Chicago. Nuzman reported observing bacillus in only one out of ten patients with Spanish flu symptoms between September and October 1918, suggesting that something else must have been causing the illness.[8]

Some doctors hypothesized that particles smaller than bacteria, what we now call viruses, might be the source. The main challenge for scientists was to figure out how to test this idea. René Dujarric de la Rivière proposed an experiment: filter all the bacteria out of the blood of flu patients and inject the remaining fluid into a person to see if the illness still developed. Who could accept this proposition, given that millions of people were dying because of this pandemic? Dujarric de la Rivière decided to test it on himself and asked his friend Lacassagne to assist him:

> Can you inject me with the filtered blood of a flu patient?[9]

Lacassagne was initially hesitant, but Dujarric convinced him by emphasizing the dire situation of humanity, and so he did it. Within a few days, Dujarric became sick. Although this method turned out to be incorrect, as the flu virus is least likely to be transmitted through blood, Dujarric was right about the existence of smaller particles.[10] It took scientists several decades to identify the exact source of the Spanish flu. The flu virus was first physically observed in 1943, 24 years after the Spanish flu had been declared over. Apparently, the speed of scientific discoveries was not as fast as it is today.

Despite its name, the Spanish flu had almost nothing to do with Spain. The only reason for the name was that Spain, being a neutral country in World War I, did not impose wartime censorship on the communication of disease information. In contrast, most other European countries were censoring the real death toll in order to sustain morale among their citizens. As a result, the pandemic is still referred to as the "Spanish flu," since the Spanish media were among the few reporting the outbreak.

Within four months of its emergence, the Spanish flu had spread globally.[11] Alfred W. Crosby, who was a professor of history, geography, and American studies at the University of Texas at Austin, says that between 1918 and 1919, an estimated 25 million Americans, more than a quarter of the population, were affected.[12] The virus primarily spread globally via military camps and ports. For example, 75,000 cases of flu were recorded in Odesa, a port in Ukraine.[13] With no known medical treatment, technique, or medicine available, doctors were practically powerless. Some of them even suggested alcohol as a remedy. This suggestion led to a surge in bourbon and whiskey sales in 1918.[14] Consequently, all the work was on the shoulders of the nurses, who provided blankets, food, and care for patients. The contagion was so pervasive that in New York, for example,

20% of the nurses contracted the flu themselves. A writer and editor at *The Pennsylvania Gazette*, Eileen A. Lynch, notes that "people turn to home remedies: goose-grease poultices, sulfur fumes, onion syrup, chloride of lime,"[15] a detail that highlights just how desperate society had become.

In the absence of a vaccine, people resorted to a range of social distancing measures or non-pharmaceutical interventions (NPIs) to curb the spread of the flu. These included wearing masks, quarantining sick people, lockdowns, and school closures. While some scientists expressed doubts about the effectiveness of these measures in controlling the pandemic, public authorities and other scientific voices strongly advocated for their adoption. Consequently, almost all cities in the U.S. adopted some version of NPIs, and 79% of the cities adopted a combination of various NPIs, which remained in place for almost a month. In October 1918, for example, the mayor of San Francisco, the Board of Health, the Red Cross, and many other public organizations published a newspaper article strongly advised that people should wear masks in public.[16] A legal ordinance was signed and went into effect in November, with police ensuring compliance and a penalty of $5 to $10 or imprisonment for transgression. Lockdowns led to financial losses for stores and companies, resulting in opposition from many people. The *New York Times* even reported that a bomb had been placed near the office of Dr. Hassler, the chief of San Francisco's Board of Health.[17]

The global implementation of these measures differed from country to country. For example, Japan did not implement similar measures to those of the United States, but Korea did (Fig. 2.2).[18]

As can be seen, the debate over the effectiveness of public health measures is nothing new; it was alive before the COVID-19 pandemic. In a 2007 analysis of 43 U.S. cities during the 1918–1919 Spanish flu, Howard Markel and his team at the University of Michigan Medical School found that those communities that acted early and maintained restrictions longer suffered far fewer deaths.[19] That same year, Richard Hatchett from the National Institute of Allergy and Infectious Diseases reached a similar conclusion in a study published in *Proceedings of the National Academy of Sciences*: cities that implemented immediate interventions following the onset of the pandemic experienced excess mortality rates (death rates above historical baselines) which were nearly 30% lower than those that did not. A more recent contribution by economist Robert J. Barro at Harvard, using excess mortality data from 45 cities, adds an important nuance. He finds that while more intensive NPIs managed to flatten the

Fig. 2.2 Spanish flu in 1918. Police officers in masks. (Source: https://commons.wikimedia.org/wiki/File:Spanish_flu_in_1918,_Police_officers_in_masks,_Seattle_Police_Department_detail,_from-_165-WW-269B-25-police-l_%28cropped%29.jpg)

mortality curve, reducing the height of the mortality peak, they did not actually reduce the cumulative number of deaths. In his reading, NPIs delayed fatalities, rather than preventing them.

Taken together, the evidence moves from clearly positive findings to more inconclusive ones about the effectiveness of NPIs in reducing mortality, though no research suggests they actively worsen outcomes. Yet one striking feature of this entire body of work is what it leaves out: the social, economic, and educational costs imposed by these measures. The mortality effects are studied in detail, but the broader aftershocks remain largely outside the frame, even though they shape livelihoods just as powerfully as the virus itself.

Historian Crosby states that influenza had killed 10 times as many American civilians as died in the World War I.[20] According to his calculations, the total number of Americans who died from Spanish influenza amounts to 550,000; in comparison, a combined total of 423,000 U.S. people died as a result of World War I, World War II, the Korean War, and the Vietnam War.[21] The flu also decreased life expectancy in America by 12 years.[22] Of course, this devastating effect was not limited to the United States. Poorer countries were hit even harder. From the available statistics, Kenya, India, and Guatemala appeared to have suffered the highest death rates relative to their populations (see Fig. 2.3). The flu's reach was global, but its toll was sharply uneven.

Several very famous people died because of the Spanish flu, including German sociologist and economist Max Weber; Frederick Trump, the grandfather of the 45th and 47th U.S. President, Donald Trump; and

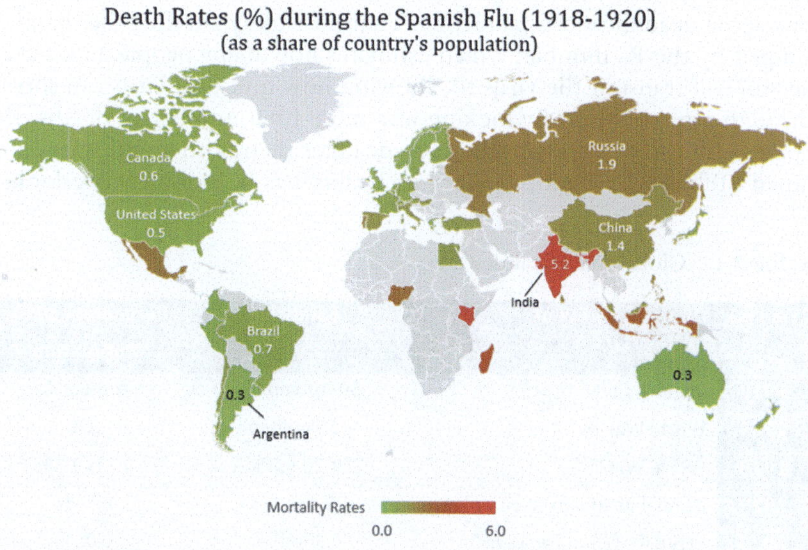

Fig. 2.3 Death rates (% of population) during the 1918–20 Spanish flu. Countries like India (5.2%), Russia (1.9%), and China (1.4%) suffered disproportionately high mortality, while others, such as Argentina, Australia, and Canada, experienced significantly lower rates. Countries shaded in gray lack available data. The color gradient from green to red reflects increasing death rates across the globe. (Source: Prepared by Orhan Erdem using data from Barro et al., 2020)

Austrian painter Gustav Klimt.[23] Robert Barro even speculates that the Spanish flu indirectly contributed to World War II. He suggests that Woodrow Wilson, then the U.S. president might have harmed the peace negotiations and thus resulted in Great Britain and France being the winners of the war, which then pushed very harsh terms on Germany during the Versailles Treaty in 1919. According to his theory, these severe terms made the German people seek revenge, contributing to the rise of the Nazis and the outbreak of World War II.

The world has faced many pandemics since 1918, including the 1957 Asian flu, the Hong Kong flu of 1968, the 1977 Russian flu, the 2002 SARS, and the 2009 swine flu, but none of them was comparable to the Spanish flu. Nicolas Christakis, director of the Human Nature Lab at Yale University, states that the Spanish flu ranks highest in terms of both severity and transmissibility among all pandemics in the past century.[24] He measures severity by a metric called case fatality rate (CFR), which is calculated by dividing the total number of deaths by all observed cases, indicating the deadliness of a pandemic. Transmissibility, on the other hand, is gauged by the R_0 number, which estimates how many people an infected person will transmit the virus to, showing how quickly a virus can spread through a population. By looking at a mere total number of deaths, the Spanish flu can be shown to be even deadlier than both world wars combined (Table 2.1). Unfortunately, its fatality has been largely overlooked

Table 2.1 Global mass fatalities

Year(s)	Event	Fatalities	Percentage of the Population
1918	Spanish flu	50-100 million	2.6-5.2%
1945	World War II	55 million	3%
1918	World War I	10-20 million	0.7%-1.4%
2019	Annual deaths from all causes	58.4 million	0.75%
2022	COVID-19 (in three years)	6.7 million	0.08%
1957	Asian flu	1-4 million	0.04-0.1%
1968	Hong Kong flu	1-4 million	0.02-0.08%
1977	Russian flu	700,000	>0.00%
2009	Swine flu (H1N1)	150-575,000	>0.00%

Source: Wikipedia, (Christakis, 2020), (Myhrvold, 2013), usafacts.com

on the shelves of history, mainly due to its occurrence shortly after World War I.

Unlike most influenza epidemics, which are characterized by a "U"-shaped mortality age profile, affecting young children and the elderly, the Spanish flu presented a "W"-shaped profile. It not only killed the very young and the old but also took a significant toll on people aged 15 to 44, thus effectively reducing the production power of countries.[25]

One of the deadliest pandemics in human history, if not the deadliest, was overshadowed by World War I. By the time the first cases of Spanish flu were reported in the United States, the war was coming to an end, and public attention was elsewhere. The victorious nations were mesmerized by the pride of their triumph. Thousands of war monuments and memorials were built in the U.S. alone.[26] In the U.S., November 11, Armistice Day, was proclaimed "Veterans Day" by President Wilson, who proudly stated:

> *To us in America, the reflections of Armistice Day will be filled with solemn pride in the heroism of those who died in the country's service and with gratitude for the victory...*[27]

Yet while the winners celebrated, the pandemic was quietly rewriting the social landscape. The Spanish flu did not strike societies evenly. Pandemics rarely do. Recent studies are now revealing evidence of this inequality. The disadvantaged were hit hardest, and the evidence is especially vivid in historical urban records.

One of the sharpest demonstrations of this comes from University of Oslo professor Svenn-Erik Mamelund's meticulous 2006 study of Kristiania (modern Oslo).[28] Mamelund did something earlier scholars did not do: He linked together individual census data, household information, and district-level characteristics for nearly 47,000 residents. Instead of relying on anecdote, "even kings and presidents got the flu," he dug through archives and explored who actually died. The logic was simple: if the disease had truly been socially neutral, then once you adjusted for age and sex, the chances of dying should roughly look similar across class lines. They did not.

He found that class mattered, wealth mattered, and place mattered. Individuals from bourgeois and middle classes had substantially lower mortality rates than members of the working class. Household space mattered too: Those living in larger apartments, four to six rooms, had about half the mortality risk of those squeezed in one-room units. Geography mattered too. Residents of Grønland-Wexels, one of the city's poorest and most crowded districts, suffered about 50% higher mortality than their counterparts in affluent Frogne.

The Spanish flu may have been a biological event, but it traveled along social fault lines. Even in 1918, the virus revealed that crises always hurt the poor and the disadvantaged more than others.

Notes

1. Porter (2008)
2. Davis (2011, p. 70)
3. Givner (1979)
4. Davis (2011)
5. Davis (2011)
6. Encyclopedia.com (2025)
7. Johnson and Mueller (2002)
8. Crosby (2003, p. 71)
9. Spinney (2017, p. 178)
10. Spinney (2017, p. 178)
11. Crosby (2003, p. 28)
12. Crosby (2003, p. 205)
13. Lynch (1998, p. 162)
14. Davis (2018, p. 164)
15. Lynch (1998)
16. Crosby (2003, p. 102)
17. Hauser (2020)
18. Spinney (2017, p. 99)
19. Markel et al. (2007)
20. Crosby (2003, p. 11)
21. Crosby (2003, p. 207)
22. Byerly (2005, p. 5)
23. Barro et al. (2020)
24. Christakis (2020, p. 64)
25. Brainerd and Siegler (2003)
26. Yuko (2021)
27. U.S. Department of Veterans Affairs (2022)
28. Mamelund (2006)

CHAPTER 3

This Time is Different (?)

Abstract This chapter critically examines the early phase of COVID-19, including its emergence, global spread, and the initial responses of governments and institutions. It questions the common belief that modern societies are fundamentally better equipped to handle pandemics, showing instead that delays, misjudgments, and information failures persisted. The chapter highlights the role of globalization in accelerating transmission and underscores how early warning signals were often ignored or underestimated, contributing to the scale of the crisis.

Keywords Preparedness • COVID-19 emergence • NPIs • Lockdowns • Policy response • Uncertainty

In 2015, a prominent public figure published a paper in the *New England Journal of Medicine*, a highly respected medical journal that has been published since 1812, in which he stated:

> There is a significant chance that an epidemic of a substantially more infectious disease will occur sometime in the next 20 years. … An epidemic is one of the few catastrophes that could set the world back drastically in the next few decades...

O. Erdem, *The Socioeconomic Impact of Pandemics*,
https://doi.org/10.1007/978-3-032-24189-4_3

Later that same year, he gave a TED talk titled "The next outbreak? We're not ready," voicing the same concerns that the greatest risk to humanity was not a nuclear war but a virus. He warned that there would be millions of deaths and trillions of dollars of economic loss were there to be a 1918-like pandemic. The TED talk was viewed by a mere 2–3 million people in the five years up to 2020. That public figure was Bill Gates. Even being one of the founders of the software giant Microsoft was not enough to draw widespread attention to his warnings.

Ed Yong is a science journalist at *The Atlantic*, known for his numerous awards and two *New York Times* bestseller books. A full century after the Spanish flu, he published an article in The Atlantic in 2018 titled "The Next Plague Is Coming. Is America Ready?" The title succinctly reflected what Yong aimed to say. He noted that the Spanish flu reduced the expected life of Americans by more than a decade and added that the total number of outbreaks per decade has been on the rise since then, increasing more than threefold since the 1980s. Yong argued that the world was not ready for a 1918-like pandemic. Citing America's various chronic problems, such as long supply chains, underfunded public health programs, and the policies of then-president Donald Trump, he concluded with a reference to the Spanish flu: "The epidemics of the early 21st century revealed a world unprepared, even as the risks continue to multiply. Much worse is coming."[1]

The paper did not sound very interesting in 2018, and it likely attracted little attention.

Similarly, in the conclusion of her 2017 book, *Pale Rider*, one of the few books dedicated to the Spanish flu, Laura Spinney posits that "What the Spanish flu taught, in essence, is that another flu pandemic is inevitable, but whether it kills 10 million or 100 million will be determined by the world into which it emerges."[2]

While not numerous, some federal institutes were also monitoring potential global threats. For example, the National Intelligence Council (NIC) had been periodically releasing reports. Well, before Gates and Yong, NIC (2004) reported that:

> ...another large-scale development that we believe could stop globalization would be a pandemic. ... Some experts believe it is only a matter of time before a new pandemic appears, such as the 1918–1919 influenza virus that killed an estimated 20 million worldwide. Such a pandemic in megacities of

> the developing world with poor health-care systems ... would be devastating and could spread rapidly throughout the world.[3]

This report mentions an estimated number of 20 million deaths globally if a pandemic of the same size were to occur.

In similar vein, the Commission on a Global Health Risk Framework for the Future (GHRF Commission), convened by the National Academy of Medicine (NAM), aimed to address the weaknesses of global health systems in their response to infectious diseases. In 2016, they published a report stating that we were likely to experience at least one pandemic in the next century and that there was at least a 20% chance that we will have four or more.[4] GHRF was also convinced of the inevitability of a pandemic.

In addition, several scientists were also raising concerns about the same problem. Following their analysis of the 2006 Swine flu pandemic, Prof. Susanna K. P. Lau and Patrick C. Y. Woo, together with numerous researchers from The University of Hong Kong, published two papers (one in 2007 and one in 2019) warning that the wet markets in China were posing a global threat.[5] They pointed out that the overcrowded cages in these markets, combined with the lack of biosecurity measures, facilitated the transmission of this virus from animals to humans. This problem, according to scientists, might lead to "devastating global outbreaks."

Following the Ebola epidemic, another body, the Global Preparedness Monitoring Board (GPMB), an independent organization that was established by the World Health Organization (WHO) and the World Bank began issuing reports on health emergencies. Their first report, released in September 2019, just a few months before the COVID-19 outbreak, seemed prescient: "The chances of a global pandemic are growing," they noted, referencing technology and science that enable the engineering of disease-causing microorganisms. They continued:

> The world is not prepared for a fast-moving, virulent respiratory pathogen pandemic. The 1918 global influenza pandemic sickened one-third of the world population and killed as many as 50 million people—2.8% of the total population. If a similar contagion occurred today ... 50–80 million people could perish. In addition to tragic levels of mortality, such a pandemic could cause panic, destabilize national security, and seriously impact the global economy and trade.[6]

Johns Hopkins University released a similar report concluding "No country is fully prepared for epidemics or pandemics, and every country has important gaps to address."[7] (According to this report, the United States is the best-prepared country for a potential epidemic, followed by the UK. However, as I will explain later, their actual readiness was compromised, mostly due to governance issues.)

Scientists warn that the number of deadly diseases jumping from animals to humans has been rising each year.[8] Every year, researchers identify two to five of these zoonotic viruses, organisms such as a virus or bacterium that originate in animals and have the potential to infect humans.[9] The World Health Organization recorded a record 1100 epidemic events worldwide between 2002 and 2007.

Emergence of COVID-19

So, by 2019, many experts and reports had consistently warned about the potential devastation of a pandemic, yet these warnings were largely ignored. The pandemic eventually emerged at the end of that year, at a moment when populist nationalism was on the rise in many countries, including the United States and the United Kingdom.

On December 1, 2019, a patient in Wuhan, China, was identified with what would later become known as COVID-19. The disease, caused by SARS-CoV-2 virus; was named after the year in which it first emerged. Dr. Jixian Zhang, the director of the Department of Respiratory Medicine of Hubei Provincial Hospital of Integrated Chinese & Western Medicine, was among the earliest physicians to alert Chinese public authorities about several abnormal pneumonia cases in her hospital. She was later awarded the National Model Worker in China.[10]

On January 11, 2020, it was announced that a 61-year-old man in the Chinese city of Wuhan had died from the novel virus. The virus spread so fast that within a week hospitals in Wuhan had reached their capacity. First, on January 23, Wuhan, with its 11 million residents, was locked down and closed to the outside world. Soon after, the surrounding cities followed.[11] This initial lockdown was crucial, as it would soon set an example for the rest of the world. At the time, Gauden Galea, the WHO's representative in China, told the *Associated Press* that "To my knowledge, trying to contain a city of 11 million people is new to science."[12] Yet China did not stop there. By the end of January, the Chinese government had implemented a full lockdown across the country. Subsequently, the Chinese city of Wuhan built a 645,000-square-foot (60,000-square-meter) hospital with thirty intensive care units in just ten days, opening it at the beginning of February."[13]

The first confirmed case outside China was reported in Thailand on January 13; it involved a traveler from Wuhan, China.[14] By the end of January, the number of reported COVID-19 cases exceeded 2000. By the end of February, this figure had reached 79,000 cases with 2500 fatalities. Stunningly, however, it took nearly four months for the World Health Organization (WHO) to assess the severity of the outbreak. On March 11, 2020, after 107,000 cases were reported and 3600 lives lost globally, the WHO officially declared COVID-19 a pandemic.

In the U.S., the situation was particularly confusing, since President Donald Trump consistently downplayed the pandemic. He repeated nine times in February and March that the coronavirus would soon "go away." On February 10, 2020, for example, he claimed, "You know, a lot of people think that goes away in April with the heat—as the heat comes in. Typically, that will go away in April."[15] Unfortunately, the virus went away neither in April nor in May, nor at any time during that year. It is also worth noting that many writers and journalists have argued that the Trump administration weakened the nation's pandemic preparedness before COVID-19 emerged. In *The Premonition*, the American author Michael Lewis writes that in April 2018, Trump's national security advisor, John Bolton, dismissed the entire staff of this unit.[16]Meanwhile, *The Washington Post* reported that the Trump administration had reduced funding for the Centers for Disease Control and Prevention (CDC), leading the agency scaled back programs aimed at preventing outbreaks in many countries it previously operated.[17]

The UK was no different. Prime Minister Boris Johnson initially downplayed the severity of the pandemic, even advising the public to "ignore it,"[18] proudly stating:

> I'm shaking hands continuously. I was at a hospital the other night where I think there were actually a few coronavirus patients and I shook hands with everybody, you'll be pleased to know. I continue to shake hands.[19]

Johnson nearly paid a high price for this approach, being admitted to the intensive care unit of St. Thomas' Hospital in London on March 23 because of persistent COVID-19 symptoms. Luckily, he recovered; unlike thousands of others.

In Brazil, President Jair Bolsonaro also followed a similar tone, dismissing the coronavirus as a media "fantasy."[20] Many of us, including myself, disagreed with these populist interpretations. Yet, our frustration often made it harder to acknowledge certain elements in the arguments of those who opposed strict lockdowns. Their view for lighter restrictions was not simple reckless improvisation; it also reflected genuine concerns about livelihoods, economic fragility, and the social costs that prolonged measures can create. The case for tighter restrictions became so dominant, and at times so emotionally charged (such as money or lives), that the voices of the dissidents were not heard enough, even when they raised concerns which were worthy of consideration.

As the world struggled with the rapid spread of a new virus, one question loomed large: where did it come from?

Source of the Pandemic

The scientific trail begins with bats, or so the prevailing hypothesis goes, but the truth remains frustratingly unclear. In the early days of the pandemic, many scientists suggested that the likely source was the Huanan Seafood Market in Wuhan, China, where vendors once sold fish and live mammals, like bats, alongside one another. For a long time, and perhaps still in the minds of many, this market has stood as the most commonly cited origin of the pandemic.

Yet, Wuhan has more than fish markets. Just a few miles away from the seafood market is the Wuhan Center for Disease Control, and, further across the river, roughly around 10 km away, the Wuhan Institute of Virology. These facilities, which study coronavirus, have become part of the second and more hotly debated narrative. By June 2021, the questions had grown loud enough that the presidents of The National Academies of Sciences, Engineering, and Medicine issued a public statement. They urged that any inquiry into the origins of SARS-CoV-2 be guided by careful evidence and scientific method, and that investigators keep in mind the full range of possibilities, from a natural spillover between animals and humans to possible links with laboratory work.[21]

The debate sharpened over the years, reaching all the way to the FBI, whose director, Christopher Wray, made a public statement in 2023, in which he stated that the bureau believed a laboratory leak to be the most likely source of the pandemic.[22] Around the same time, a not-yet-peer-reviewed study added fuel to the controversy. Analyzing the virus's genetic code, the researchers argued that certain features were unusually consistent with methods commonly used in laboratory research.

The conversation spilled beyond the lab. Mustafa Suleyman, CEO of Microsoft AI, reflected in his co-authored 2023 book that whatever happened in Wuhan, the mere possibility of a research-related escape should trouble us.[23] A year later, Richard H. Ebright, a molecular biologist at Rutgers University, testified to the U.S. Senate in June 2024 that COVID-19 most likely originated from a lab-related incident in Wuhan rather than a natural spillover. He pointed to its emergence far from bat populations, lax lab safety, genetic features consistent with engineered viruses, and the absence of any proven animal host as key evidence.[24] Unfortunately, as at the time I was drafting this book, Chinese authorities persist in their reluctance to cooperate with the international community in investigating the origins of the virus.

And still, firm answers to questions are vague. While the exact origin of SARS-CoV-2 remains unresolved, one thing is clear: even though the idea of a biological threat, whether accidental or deliberate, was initially dismissed, this possibility cannot be entirely ruled out. The pandemic has shown that such threats might endanger humanity in the future.

The Virus Crosses Borders

By the time governments began canceling flights to and from China, the virus had already spread beyond borders. Reports of infected people in other countries began to emerge. Soon, many countries started implementing various forms of non-pharmaceutical interventions (NPIs), which include wearing masks, closing schools, canceling public events, lockdowns, and quarantines, among others.

On March 9, Italy became the first country after China to introduce lockdowns. The virus had struck the northern part of the country with extraordinary speed and severity, particularly in Lombardy and Veneto. Hospitals in Bergamo and Milan were soon overwhelmed.

While the rest of the world was still considering what to do, and how to do it, on March 16, a group of scientists led by Neil Ferguson from Imperial College London released a report.[25] They projected that, without intervention, approximately 510,000 people in the UK, and 2.2 million in the U.S., could die. The study concluded that only strict, sustained suppression measures, such as nationwide social distancing, isolation, and school closures, could prevent health systems from being overwhelmed and thereby avert these catastrophic death tolls. This report was circulated among academics and policymakers alike, and had a huge impact on the decisions made thereafter.

Soon afterward, almost all other countries (except for a few outliers, such as Sweden, discussed below) around the world began implementing various versions of lockdown measures, including Spain on March 16 and the UK on March 23. Worldwide, stores and schools were closed, and public events were called off. By late March and early April, more than 3.9 billion people, about half of the world's population, were under government-ordered lockdowns or quarantine.[26] Among the 180 countries monitored by the Oxford COVID-19 Government Response Tracker (OxCGRT), only 7 countries had not implemented any form of NPI by the end of March 2020. This was an unprecedented global experiment, an attempt to contain a virus by keeping nearly the entire world indoors.

In the United States, many people, including me, took extreme precautions, used N95 masks in indoor spaces, kept six feet of distance in public, and disinfected every grocery item brought home. We were advised to do so. At one point, widespread caution led people to stockpile toilet paper to such an extent that it created a nationwide shortage. I remember attending an estate sale in Illinois in 2021 and discovering that the seller had filled half a room with rolls of toilet paper, which they were now trying to sell off. Schools and universities were quickly closed, with teachers and instructors delivering their lessons remotely from home.

Research published during these early days of the pandemic generally supported the imposition of strong NPIs. For example, a widely cited study in *Nature,* one of the world's leading scientific journals, offered one of the first global attempts to measure how government interventions, such as travel restrictions, school closures, business shutdowns, and stay-at-home orders, slowed the spread of COVID-19.[27] Drawing on early data from countries hit hard in 2020, such as China, South Korea, Italy, Iran, France, and the United States, the authors compared infection growth rates before and after policies were introduced. They concluded that without these interventions, millions of people would likely have been infected. Even though the study offered valuable evidence during an uncertain time, its claim of "millions of cases avoided" depends on the assumptions about how the virus would have spread without intervention, a modeled scenario rather than an observable counterfactual.

For the first time in U.S. history, all 55 governors declared emergencies simultaneously in response to the same crisis.,[2829] In 2020 and 2021, state legislatures passed at least 70 bills related to governors' and health officials' emergency powers.

Yet, the nation's NPI responses were largely shaped by the political tendencies of the states. People mostly supported the measures their local authorities put in place. The first U.S. test of remote learning began on March 5, when Washington's 24,000-student Northshore district closed schools and shifted to online learning.[30] California's governor, Gavin Newsom, was the first to issue a stay-at-home order (on March 19). Soon after, all 24 Democratic governors had enacted similar measures in their states, while 19 of the 26 Republican governors did the same. However, seven Republican states, Alaska, Iowa, Nebraska, North Dakota, South Dakota, Utah, and Wyoming, never implemented a stay-at-home order.[31] Duration also varied along party lines, with governors in Democratic-led states keeping the orders in place for an average of 73 days, whereas Republican-led states maintained them for only 28 days.[32]

By the end of April 2020, the United States, together with Italy, Spain, and the United Kingdom, was among the worst-performing countries in the world, with the highest death toll per million.[33]

Certain countries stood out in a positive sense during the early phase of the pandemic. In Latin America, Cuba diverged positively by deploying door-to-door health surveillance, intensive contact tracing, and isolation, using its large physician network, which gives it the highest doctor-to-patient ratio in the world. As a result, its early outcomes were notably better than regional peers in early 2020.[34] By August 2020, Cuba had recorded only 87 deaths nationwide.[35] In contrast, among its regional peers, Mexico had reported nearly 60,000 deaths, while Peru had recorded 52,000 deaths.

Several East Asian countries, including Vietnam and South Korea, also performed comparatively well in the initial stages. Vietnam, despite its geographical proximity to China, did not record its first COVID-19-related fatality until August 1, 2020. On the same date South Korea had 298 deaths. The early success of South Korea is often attributed to the institutional memory of the 2003 SARS outbreak. Having been severely affected at that time, the country drew clear lessons, investing in public health, rapid testing capacity, and early intervention mechanisms, which enabled them to respond swiftly.[36]

The Ones Who Sounded the Alarm

Coming back to the people who warned us:

Bill Gates's talk, which was viewed by just a few million people over 5 years, gained an additional 43 million views after 2020, the year of COVID-19's global spread. He later wrote a book, entitled *How to Prevent the Next Pandemic*, which was published in 2022. As of November 2023, the book has received only 1714 ratings on Goodreads. The contrast is telling: warnings attract little attention before a crisis, immense attention during it, and surprisingly little sustained interest afterward.

Journalist Ed Yong received the Pulitzer Prize in Explanatory Reporting in 2021, one year after the emergence of the pandemic. The award, one of the most prestigious in journalism, recognizes journalists who provide clear and understandable explanations for complex subjects through mastery in their area and lucid writing. Yong later went onto receive many other notable awards, including the George Polk Award and the Benton Award, among others.

Professor Susanna K. P. Lau and Professor Patrick C. Y. Woo, the authors of the papers that warned about the Chinese wet market, are still teaching at the Department of Microbiology at The University of Hong Kong, without having any received any rewards or appreciation.

The tone of the Global Preparedness Monitoring Board (GPMB)'s 2020 report conveyed a clear "we-warned-you" message. The report's foreword begins with these words:

> "Never before has the world been so clearly forewarned of the dangers of a devastating pandemic, nor previously had the knowledge, resources, and technologies to deal with such a threat. Yet, never before has the world witnessed a pandemic of such widespread and destructive social and economic impact." [They continued], "The rapid spread of this novel coronavirus (SARS-CoV-2) has had a devastating impact which we will feel for years to come."[37]

Aftermath

COVID-19 ranks as the second most severe and highly transmissible pandemic since 1900, behind only the Spanish flu. An estimated 6.7 million lives were lost due to the pandemic between 2020 and 2022, with 1 million of those fatalities occurring in the United States alone.[38] Adam Tooze, the author of the book *Shutdown*, which summarizes how COVID-19 impacted the world economy, draws a striking parallel: Between 2020 and 2023, a significantly higher percentage of the UK population died from COVID-19 than the percentage killed by German bombs during World War II.[39]

There is a more important and deeply troubling reality: The COVID-related deaths were not evenly distributed across racial, socioeconomic, and income groups. As individuals in lower-income brackets often work in less safe environments, tend to live in substandard and crowded housing, and have limited access to preventive measures, they are more prone to infections. In the U.S., COVID-19 disproportionately harmed particularly non-Hispanic American Indian and Alaska Native (AIAN), Hispanic, and Black populations.[40] According to one measure, Hispanic people experienced mortality rates 5 times as high as White people, while mortality rates among Black people were 3 times as high as those for White people.[41]

Data from the rest of the world, including countries from Europe, Africa, and Asia, show similar results. A 2023 study in *Frontiers in Public Health* analyzed 190,485 hospitalized COVID-19 patients in Colombia and found that higher poverty levels were strongly associated with increased mortality. Patients from more deprived regions faced 1.4 to 1.7 times higher odds of death compared to those from the least impoverished areas.[42] Complementing these findings, researchers from Newcastle University conducted a comprehensive review of 95 studies worldwide and concluded that regions with greater socioeconomic disadvantage consistently experienced higher COVID-19 mortality rates than wealthier areas.[43] Nearly all the studies point to the same conclusion: COVID-19 disproportionately impacted economically disadvantaged people. Addressing this deep disparity will take a lot of time, if it can ever be fully resolved.

The ripple effects of COVID-19 extended far beyond the tragic toll of 6.7 million lives lost. In a 2024 study published in Science, researchers followed COVID-19 patients for a year and found that those suffering from Long Covid showed persistent immune abnormalities. Instead of returning to normal after infection, part of the immune system remained overactive, accompanied by signs of inflammation, tissue damage, and abnormal blood clotting.[44] Another study revealed that SARS-CoV-2 has lasting health consequences, identifying 36 distinct long-term effects, such as viral pneumonia, acute myocarditis, and malnutrition, among over

1.37 million COVID-19 survivors in the U.S.[45] The pandemic transformed politics, education, technology, and health administration and altered people's perspectives on religion, leaving irreversible marks on society. These topics will be explored further in the second part of the book.

On Stringency

NPIs, such as social distancing, mask-wearing, school-closures, and bans on public gatherings, became one of the most controversial aspects of the pandemic. Scientists, journalists, and the public were sharply divided not only over the effectiveness of these NPIs but also with regard to how to weigh their costs. The divide persists.

I remember travelling with my family, from Illinois to Yellowstone, passing through four different states, Wisconsin, Minnesota, South Dakota, and Wyoming, each governed by its own political outlook. In Wisconsin, almost no one wore masks, and people looked at us with a hint of confusion or curiosity. Later, after crossing into Minnesota, the scene flipped completely: everyone wore masks. The pattern repeated as we moved westward. It was a live demonstration of how a single country could contain radically different understandings of the same guidance.

Even mainstream media reflected this division. In 2023, he *New York Times* published two op-eds just 17 days apart: one dismissing masks as useless,[46] the other praising their effectiveness.[47] There is an extensive body of research claiming the effectiveness of measures such as mask-wearing and social distancing, while studies arguing the opposite are far fewer in number.[48] Yet what remained strikingly absent from much of this debate was a systematic accounting of trade-offs. As Walter Scheidel, an economic historian at Stanford University, put it at the time: "Why is nobody putting some numbers on the economic costs of a … shutdown against the lives saved? The whole discipline is well equipped for it. But there is some reluctance…".[49]

How about those countries that adopted far fewer NPIs? How did their outcomes compare? One particularly illustrative case is Sweden, once described during the pandemic as "Scandinavia's pariah state."

"Scandinavia's Pariah State": Sweden

Sweden selected a path that set it apart from nearly all of Europe, and also the rest of the world. The country's first case of COVID-19 was observed on January 31, and the first death on March 11, the date when the Swedish government announced a ban on public gatherings of more than 500, in common with the approach of most other governments did.[50] On the same day Denmark closed its schools; the following day so did Norway. While nearly all of Europe had shut down, Sweden's restaurants, primary schools, gyms, and shops remained open. Swedish authorities continued to urge citizens to maintain distance, avoid international travel, wash their hands regularly, and follow basic precautions. When it came to mass lockdowns and school closures, a big national debate was already underway.

In Sweden, the legal responsibility for managing and communicating infectious-disease control lies with the Public Health Agency of Sweden, rather than with elected ministers. According to Sweden's constitutional framework, the agency operates independently from direct government intervention, a form of institutional autonomy somewhat comparable to the independence of the Federal Reserve in the United States, where the latter body sets policy to control inflation.[51] During 2020, the Swedish government, including the prime minister, consistently deferred to the agency. The prime minister made only limited public appearances, offering a handful of interviews, and no crisis group was formed in the Parliament.[52] As a result, much of the responsibility rested on the shoulders of the agency, whose public face throughout the crisis was the state epidemiologist Anders Tegnell.

"Having a very abrupt stop of the spread now would actually move the problem ahead of us," Tegnell said. Under his guidance, and unlike their neighbors, Sweden chose to keep open the preschools or elementary schools. "It would cost more than it would give," said Education Minister Anna Ekström, defending the decision to keep younger students in classrooms.[53]

Public health advice merely urged people to keep their distance, stay home if sick, and work remotely when possible, without any mandates being enforced. Unlike most countries, Sweden did not mandate masks, impose stay-at-home orders, or enforce strict social distancing. Instead, the government relied heavily on voluntary measures and advised those who were ill or elderly to stay at home. It kept compulsory schools and nearly all businesses open.[54]

On March 17, 2020, the Swedish government recommended that upper secondary schools, colleges, and universities move to remote learning starting the next day, while elementary and preschools were to remain open.[55] The same day, Dr. Ferguson's report, which had projected 510,000 deaths in the UK and 2.2 million in the U.S., reached the Swedish authorities. Agency authorities and Tegnell thought the report's methodology was flawed, and they didn't change their mind.

Tegnell was far from alone in his views. He enjoyed broad public support, though he also had outspoken critics. Supporters even put up his posters around to show their backing for him. Some went further, arguing that Sweden's approach was actually too restrictive. Swedish financier Kerstin Hessius, who led AP3, one of Sweden's largest public pension funds, wrote an article, which basically said unemployment was rising by the second, and that prolonged restrictions could lead to mass unemployment, echoing that experienced by Germany in the 1920s or by the U.S. in the 1930s. She urged the government to set a clear timetable for ending the current state of emergency, cautioning that "an entire generation is losing its future" and that society "cannot remain in this state indefinitely." She implicitly said that the policy response should focus not only on the disease but also on the economic side, on jobs, livelihood, and generational equity.[56]

Across most of Europe, restaurants and cafés were shut down, while Sweden merely urged citizens to avoid crowds and long queues. In Germany and the United Kingdom, no more than two people were allowed to meet in public, whereas Sweden's limit was set at an astonishing 500. While many European countries closed their ski resorts, including those in the Alps across France, Switzerland, Austria, and Italy, Sweden kept its open.[57]

Viktor Barth-Kron, a commentator for the Swedish newspaper *Expressen*, captured the situation in his March 25, 2020, column titled "The Government Is Playing High, It Could End in Fiasco" as follows:

> "Either we can cope with the crisis better than comparable countries, or at least not worse. In that situation, Anders Tegnell is likely to be the new Hans Rosling and Stefan Löfven will emerge as Europe's coolest prime minister ... Or Sweden is doing worse than its more restrictive neighboring countries. To put it mildly, a completely different debate awaits."[58]

The differences were not just confined to schools; Sweden stood out as an exception during the pandemic. It chose not to implement most of the NPIs that were widely adopted by the international community. According to Tegnell, Sweden's strategy focused on targeting "a slow spread of infection, and [ensuring] that the health services have a reasonable workload." Lisa Brouwers, who was the head of unit for analysis in the Department of Public Health Analysis in Sweden, noted that closing schools in Spain prompted wealthy families to go to their vacation homes in coastal regions, effectively relocating the virus from schools to coasts.[59] Officials argued that stopping the virus was impossible; regardless of the measures taken, the death toll would be similar across countries one year after the onset of the pandemic.[60] For this reason, they viewed the heavy social and economic costs of lockdown as being unjustified. Their guiding principle was "to reduce the pace, not reduce at any cost."[61] Their approach rested on managing, rather than suppressing, the spread.

In July 2020, the European Centre for Disease Prevention and Control (ECDC) recommended that people should wear masks in public places. Yet that same month, the percentage of people wearing masks in France or Germany was about five times higher than in Sweden.[62] Therefore, Sweden's unorthodox approach drew international criticism; the *New York Times* even described the country as "Scandinavia's pariah state."[63]

Early analyses during the pandemic judged Sweden's COVID-19 approach as being largely unsuccessful and even described it as a "scientifically questionable" and "dangerous" fallacy, an assessment that was partially accurate by then.[64] In that context, such criticism was understandable: policymakers were operating under severe uncertainty, vaccines did not yet exist, and governments around the world were under intense pressure to save lives. Five years later, however, the outcomes allow for a clearer and more balanced assessment of both Sweden's strategy and the broader role of non-pharmaceutical interventions (NPIs) during the pandemic. With the benefit of hindsight, we can now examine what NPIs achieved, what costs they imposed, and whether those costs were justified.

The NPI Dilemma

NPIs were designed to protect societies from viral spread, yet they also disrupted schooling, consumption, employment, education, and daily life in profound ways. After almost five years, the NPI debate can be boiled down to two main questions:

1. Did NPIs work?
2. Even if they did, were the costs worth bearing? Or are we sure that there are not any other, less costly ways to achieve the same benefit?

If the answers to both of these questions are yes, then we can call the strategy efficient.

I will not attempt to assess the effectiveness of each measure individually; rather, I aim to reflect on the broader societal practice of NPIs, how effective they were as a collective strategy, and how their benefits compared with their costs. This balance was largely defined by two opposing forces: protection and disruption. Some might argue, "What's wrong with excessive NPIs? If we don't implement them, people die; if we do and they prove unnecessary, what harm is done?" Yet this view is deeply flawed, because every implementation, however well-intentioned, carries its own costs. Measures that protect society from infection can simultaneously fracture its normal functioning, disrupting education, livelihoods, and social cohesion in ways that may continue long after the virus. School closures may have slowed viral transmission, but they also interrupted education, widened inequality, and prevented younger generations from socializing and learning. Lockdowns, meanwhile, protected many households from exposure but forced some businesses to shut down and brought many economic activities to a halt. They also reshaped patterns of medical care: many patients with other serious conditions hesitated to visit hospitals, delaying diagnoses and treatments that, under normal conditions, would never have been postponed.

To avoid contemporary political pressures, it is helpful to begin with research conducted before COVID-19. Two of the most valuable come from 2007, when researchers revisited the 1918 Spanish flu with no modern agenda to defend.

The first, by Howard Markel and colleagues from the University of Michigan, stands out in this regard. They found that during the 1918 flu pandemic layered and sustained NPIs, especially school closures and bans on public gatherings, were associated with slower peaks and substantially lower overall mortality across 43 U.S. cities. Cities that acted sooner and kept measures in place longer saw markedly fewer deaths. This remains one of the strongest pieces of historical evidence suggesting that NPIs can slow viral spread.[65] A companion study by three researchers, Hatchett, Mecher, and Lipsitch, painted the same picture in even sharper relief. Looking closely at the experience in 17 cities, they showed that early, stacked interventions could cut peak death rates by nearly half. Their comparison of Philadelphia and St. Louis has since become almost mythic: Philadelphia allowed a parade to go forward despite early signs of trouble, while St. Louis shut down public gatherings within days. The outcomes diverged dramatically; one city was overwhelmed, the other shaken but far less shattered.[66] Yet, like all historical work, many interventions occurred simultaneously, and no single measure can be cleanly isolated. The main limitation of both papers is that the analyses are correlational rather than causally identified; despite that constraint, however, they offer compelling evidence.

To evaluate the impact of NPIs on lives saved, one approach is to compare the death rates of countries with varying levels of strictness, as measured by the University of Oxford's COVID-19 Government Response Tracker project (or OxCGRT).[67] This would allow us to explore whether implementing stricter NPIs is correlated with low levels of death. The OxCGRT project compiles various policy indicators covering school closures and travel bans, health, and economic policies for each country. Nine of these indicators form a composite measure, which is known as the Stringency Index.

This index quantifies the intensity of a country's response to COVID-19 over time.[68] The index ranges from 0 (lightest response) and 100 (strictest response). Higher values on the index reflect more stringent national responses. Over time, the index traces a global experiment in crisis management, revealing just how differently governments reacted to the same virus.

According to OxCGRT's Stringency Index, while many developed countries, such as the U.S., Germany, Spain, and the UK, were slow in their response, emerging and underdeveloped countries such as India, South Africa, China, and Peru responded more quickly. Peru, in particular, stands out: it implemented some of the most stringent lockdowns in the world. Its average Stringency Index ranked sixth highest globally in the world in 2020 and remained among the top 21 when averaging across the entire 2020–2022 period. China recorded the highest average stringency levels over these three years, while Sweden, often cited as an outlier, ranked near the bottom.

If stricter policies reliably saved more lives, these stark contrasts in government responses should be reflected in similar differences in mortality. To explore this, we can compare cumulative COVID-19 deaths per million, using the end of 2023 as a common reference point. The resulting

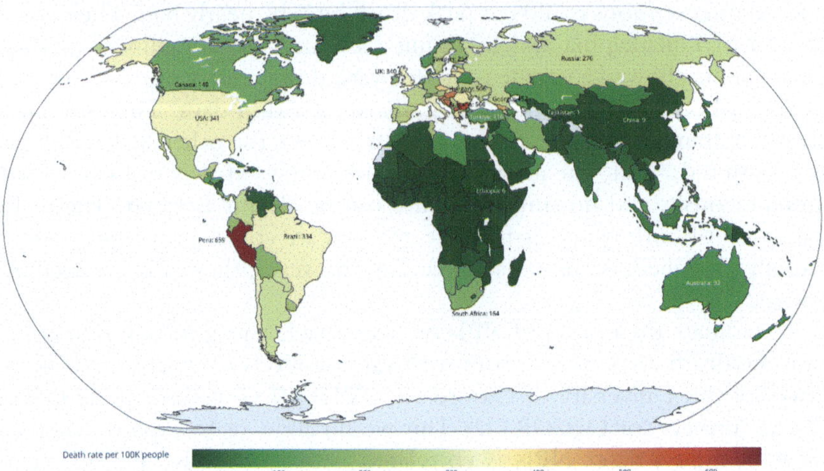

Fig. 3.1 COVID-19 death rates per 100,000 people (December 2023). Each country is shaded from green (≈ 0 deaths per 100,000 people) to dark red (> 500 deaths per 100,000), with labels on selected nations. The map highlights the difference across regions: Peru (659), Brazil (334), the United States (341), and Russia (276) recorded some of the highest death rates, while countries like China (9) and Tajikistan (1) remained at the lower end of the scale. Source: ourworldindata.org

picture is anything but simple. By December 31, 2023, Peru had recorded the highest cumulative death rates in the world, at roughly 659 per 100,000 people. Bulgaria, Bosnia and Herzegovina, and Hungary followed, with rates of 566, 511, and 306, respectively. At the other end of the spectrum were countries such as Tajikistan, Uzbekistan, Ethiopia, and China, which reported extremely low cumulative death rates. Sweden, despite its relatively light approach, ended up having a death of 254, neither among the highest nor among the lowest group, but roughly in between (see Fig. 3.1).

When these patterns are summarized formally, the relationship between policy strictness and mortality nearly disappears. Across countries, the correlation between average stringency during 2020–2022 and total deaths per million by the end of 2023 is weak and statistically insignificant ($r=0.08$, $p=0.31$). In other words, countries that imposed the harshest restrictions did not systematically experience lower death rates, and nor did those with lighter approaches inevitably have high death rates.

This comparison reveals an uncomfortable but important point. China and Peru, two countries that adopted sharply different levels of NPI stringency, ultimately ended up on opposite ends of the mortality spectrum. Peru recorded one of the highest death rates globally, while China reported one of the lowest. The contrast suggests that stringency, by itself, was never a strategy.

Policies operate within societies, not above them. Their effectiveness ultimately depends on how people respond, a response shaped by cultural norms, social expectations, and trust. In practice, implementation is inseparable from the institutional, social, and economic environments within which policies are applied. Compliance matters, and compliance, in turn, is deeply influenced by culture and trust. In Peru, only about 11% of the population reports having "a great deal" or "quite a lot" of confidence in their government. In China, this figure is close to 95%.[69] This difference alone suggests that similar rules would translate into very different real-world behavior.

Peru's experience illustrates the limits of severity in the absence of institutional support. The country locked down early and aggressively, yet other factors, such as structural healthcare problems, widespread informal employment, and limited social safety nets, undermined the effectiveness of those measures. Peru had invested very little in its healthcare system for years; in fact, it had one of the lowest levels of public health spending in all of Latin America.[70] As one observer noted, the government's lockdown effectively worked only for the 30% of Peruvians in the formal sector. For the remaining 70%, who lack basic health services, education, and nutrition, compliance was far less feasible.[71] In the end, Peru's experience illustrates how NPIs can falter when the surrounding social and institutional foundations are too weak to support them. China, by contrast, enforces one of the most stringent lockdowns in the world, enabled by high state capacity and strong compliance.

Reported COVID-19 deaths, however, are an imperfect metric. Difference in reporting practices, historical records, and data transparency complicate direct cross-country comparisons. For this reason, a more informative way to assess the human cost of the pandemic is excess mortality: the number of deaths above expected levels based on historical patterns.

The idea dates back to John Graunt's 1662 analysis of London's Bills of Mortality, where he compared epidemic deaths with normal yearly ones. Using this method, he revealed "excess" mortality. He published his observations in his book *Natural and Political Observations Made Upon the Bills of Mortality*. Today, excess mortality remains central in epidemiology because it captures both direct and indirect deaths and avoids reliance on official cause-of-death classifications. Expressed by 100,000 people, it allows comparisons across countries of different sizes and baseline mortality levels. Several institutions estimate excess mortality, one of the most widely cited being *The Economist*.[72]

By the end of 2023, *The Economist*'s global excess-mortality estimates read like a map of social divides. Serbia, Lithuania, Bulgaria, and Russia sat at the top of the list, having the heaviest death tolls, while Peru ranked 11th. Sweden, by contrast, ranked toward the bottom of the list (137th) in cumulative excess deaths, with an estimated 173 excess deaths per 100,000 people. At the bottom of the list was Greenland, which recorded negative excess mortality.[73]

Across countries, average policy strictness over 2020–2023 shows little relationship with excess mortality (Fig. 3.2). Nations with similar average restrictions experience dramatically different outcomes, while some countries with relatively modest restrictions recorded low excess mortality, and others with prolonged strictness did not. The overall relationship between average stringency and excess mortality is negligible ($r = 0.01$, $p = 0.95$), suggesting that policy severity, on average, was associated neither with fewer nor with more deaths.

This does not imply that public health measures were irrelevant or unnecessary. Rather, it underscores a reality: the long-run human toll of the pandemic was shaped by a complex interaction of factors, including demographics, baseline health, timing of interventions, institutional capacity, social behavior, and medical response. Severity without these factors did not guarantee better outcomes. The global experience suggests that how and when policies were implemented mattered at least as much as how strict they ultimately became.

This intuition is reinforced by a comprehensive analysis by Margherita Pizzato and her colleagues. Tracking excess mortality rates as a percentage above historical baselines, rather than per 100,000 people, across 29 European countries between 2020 and 2023, they show that Eastern Europe (Bulgaria, the Czech Republic, Hungary, Poland and Slovakia), suffered the highest relative excess mortality (+13.2%). This figure was

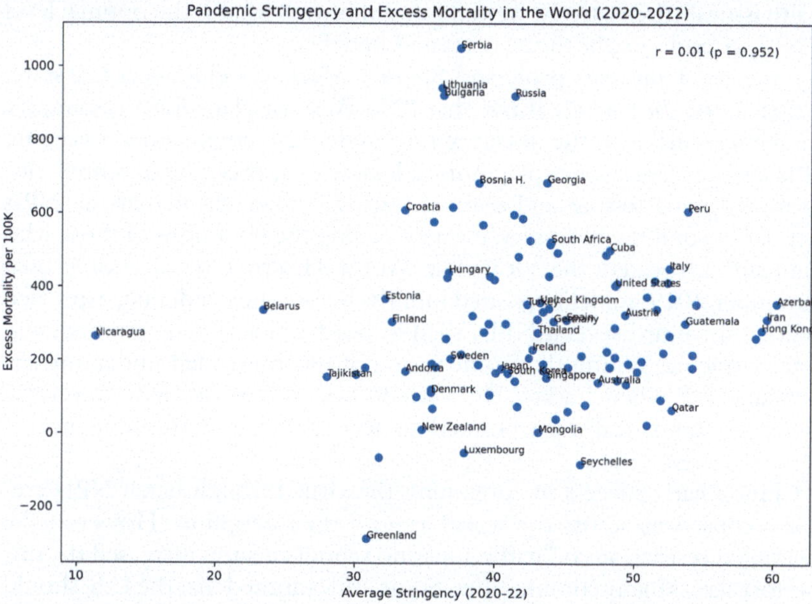

Fig. 3.2 Countries' Stringency Indices and deaths per million. Each point in this chart represents a country. The horizontal axis reports the average COVID-19 policy stringency index over the 2020–2022 period, while the vertical axis shows excess mortality per 100,000 people relative to historical baselines, as the end of 2023. The relationship is negligible (r = 0.01, p = 0.95), indicating no systematic association between average policy stringency and excess mortality across countries. Source: (Karlinsky & Kobak, 2021) and ourworldindata.org

well above Western (6.3%), Northern (7%), or Southern Europe (7.8%), with Sweden recording the lowest mortality among all European countries. Yet, the decisive factor was not how hard government pushed the NPI measures. Once demographics and long-term trends are taken into account, policy stringency fades from view. What remains are the deeper structural factors: income inequality and poverty amplifying the death toll, and wealth, health expenditure, and vaccination doing the opposite. In the end, resilience mattered more than severity.[74]

Even if we assume that the NPIs were effective, a point still debated, a more vital question remains: were they worth the social and economic costs, including declines in GDP, setbacks in education, and rising mental health issues? Alternatively, we can put it this way: what is the optimal level of NPI, considering both the costs and benefits?

Princeton University professors Stephen Macedo and Frances Lee state, in their book *In Covid's Wake*, that "No Western plans for a respiratory pandemic available at the outset of the pandemic recommended sweeping NPIs such as large-scale quarantines, lockdowns, preemptive school closures, and mass testing and contact tracing." They claim that the NPIs went far beyond the necessary, even exceeding the intentions of those who originally advocated the idea. The World Health Organization's own November 2019 guideline, issued months before the pandemic, expressed skepticism toward several NPIs, such as border closures, quarantine, and contact-tracing, noting that some were not recommended under any circumstances.[75] When I asked Dr. Macedo how the world came to reverse course so dramatically, he pointed to fear, panic, and the influence of China.[76]

China's early success in containing the virus through harsh NPIs created a consensus across the world around their adoption. However, the prolonged restrictions on gatherings and school closures increased the discomfort across many communities. Some critics argued that the U.S. should have moved from total lockdowns and instead adopted a more targeted strategy. Given that most people, especially the young and healthy, face little risk of dying from COVID-19, they contended that strict protection of vulnerable groups, targeted isolation, and reopening society would have better balanced saving lives with minimizing broader harms.[77] In fact, the UK's Office for National Statistics (ONS) reported in January 2021 that the average age of coronavirus fatalities in England and Wales was 80.3 years.[78] Thus, COVID-19 mortality was concentrated among the older adults.

With few exceptions, from March 2020, nearly all countries implemented the same blanket lockdowns and the same NPIs. Yet it was already clear that the most vulnerable group was the elderly. So why not adopt a tailored approach that varied by country? Africa, for example, had a much younger population than Europe, and in countries such as Italy and Spain a large share of older adults lived in multigenerational households. As Dr. Sucharit Bhakdi, Professor Emeritus of Medical Microbiology at the Johannes Gutenberg University Mainz, stated in his open letter to German Chancellor Angela Merkel, 27.4% of Italy's vulnerable population and 33.5% of Spain's lived with younger people, compared with just 7% in Germany.[79] Taken together, these differences suggest that the costs and

Table 3.1 Excess mortality and annual GDP growth in selected Nordic countries, 2020–2023

Countries	*2020*		*2021*		*2022*		*2023*	
	Ex Mort	*GDP (%)*	*Ex Mort*	*GDP (%)*	*Ex Mort*	*GDP (%)*	*Ex Mort*	*GDP (%)*
Denmark	2	−2.1	38	6.9	70	0.7	42	1.7
Finland	26	−2.6	59	2.5	155	0.5	112	−1.4
Germany	52	−4.2	86	3.6	135	0.6	81	−0.4
Norway	5	−1.9	32	3.4	102	2.3	66	−1.1
Sweden	85	−2.7	27	5.3	60	0.8	60	−0.6

Source: The Economist and World Bank

"Ex Mort" shows excess mortality rates (per 100,000 people), whereas GDP (%) indicates annual GDP growth.

benefits of stringent NPIs vary widely across countries, and that a uniform approach may not always be optimal. A strict lockdown in Africa risked devastating the economy while offering less benefit, and similar arguments could be made when comparing Germany and Spain.

Sweden's trajectory stands out clearly in Table 3.1, which compares it with that of its Nordic neighbors, Norway, Denmark, and Finland, as well as Germany. By the end of 2020, Sweden's excess mortality had reached 85 deaths per 100,000, far exceeding the rest of the comparable countries in the table and reflecting the country's unusual pandemic strategy. Yet its economy shrank by only 2.7%, roughly comparable to others in the region. In 2021, the picture flips: excess mortality drops to 27, the lowest in the group, while GDP growth surges to 5.3%. That combination almost looks like the delayed payoff of early exposure.

By 2022 and 2023, Sweden settles into the Nordic middle. Excess mortality rises to 60 in 2022 and stays there in 2023, neither catastrophic nor exemplary. GDP growth moderates as well, hovering around 0.8% in 2022 and being slightly negative in 2023. The wild swings of the early pandemic years give way to a steady, unremarkable pattern.

Taken together, this four-year window captures the core tension of Sweden's pandemic experiment. The country paid a price up front, rebounded both economically and in public health metrics, and ultimately converged toward the same equilibrium as its neighbors. This pattern suggests that Sweden's strategy cannot be dismissed outright as a failure, even if it hardly qualifies as a triumph.

While these measures were recommended to contain the outbreak, they would also lead to soaring unemployment rates. Indeed, many countries faced historic highs in economic indicators such as unemployment rates and GDP growth rates, the latter being a common measure of economic activity. Most of the economies experienced shocks of a magnitude not witnessed in decades, if not in centuries. Due to containment measures such as lockdowns and the prohibition of public gatherings, the pandemic brought the global economies close to a collapse, with world GDP shrinking by 2.9%—a worse decline than the 1.3% contraction during the 2007–2009 financial crisis. Britain's GDP declined by 10.3% in 2020, the biggest decline since the 1700s.[80] In the second quarter of 2020, the U.S. experienced the lowest quarterly GDP growth, at –7.5%, since the Federal Reserve began recording this data in 1948. The U.S. annual GDP contracted by 2.2% in 2020. Meanwhile, European countries faced graver circumstances. The collective GDP of the European Union contracted by 5.6%. Using data from the start of the pandemic until April 2020, that is, the first phase of COVID-19, three World Bank economists, Demirgüç-Kunt, Lokshin, and Torre, showed that the NPIs led to an approximate 10% decline in economic activity in Europe/Central Asia.[81]

However, a study published in the *European Journal of Clinical Investigation* analyzed ten countries during the spring of 2020, and found no evidence that countries implementing "more restrictive" NPIs, such as stay-at-home orders and business closures, reduced their COVID-19 case growth more than Sweden and South Korea, which were categorized as having "less restrictive" NPIs.[82] Additionally, some authoritarian governments used pandemics as an excuse to expand their surveillance and tighten control over public life. Their interventions reached into many areas, often far beyond those concerned with public health. And history shows that once the governments extend their reach, they are slow to retreat. Critics also argued that NPIs restricted individual freedoms and were therefore unlawful. I will explore this aspect of COVID-19-related restrictions in the chapter, "Politically Yours." Meanwhile, scientists have been attempting to determine the effect of early interventions on saved lives and the economy, aiming to draw lessons for future pandemics.

Compliance was another issue, as Peru's case illustrated. Ordinary people aside, hundreds of politicians who imposed the lockdowns were caught breaking their own laws. In New Zealand, for example, the health minister publicly admitted to breaching the lockdown by driving his family to a beach and later to a mountain-bike trail.[83] In the United Kingdom, Neil

Ferguson, the epidemiologist whose modelling shaped the lockdown strategy of Britain and many other countries, resigned after allowing a woman with whom he was in a relationship to visit his home, not just once but twice, in violation of the very guidelines he helped craft.[84] Similarly, in New York, Mayor Bill de Blasio drew similar criticism after continuing to visit his neighborhood gym in mid-March 2020, even as his administration urged residents to stay home and avoid exactly that kind of nonessential activity.[85] These kinds of behaviors undermined public trust and showed how fragile compliance could become during strict lockdown measures.

There are also other side effects. Macmillan Cancer Support, a UK charity, for example, warned that around 50,000 cancer cases went undiagnosed, and about 33,000 treatments were delayed, during COVID-19 disruptions. Even operating above full capacity, it would take years to clear the backlog.[86] France also reported similar figures about undetected cancer patients.[87]

Optimal Stringency

In the previous chapter (and partially in the coming chapters), we saw the central paradox of pandemic policy: measures strict enough to suppress a virus can simultaneously harm the society they aim to protect. I will cover some other harms, such as economics and education, in the coming chapters. Countries that acted aggressively sometimes succeeded, sometimes failed; countries, such as Sweden, that did little sometimes fared well, sometimes performed disastrously. Thus, the evidence is mixed. A strategy that works well in some state might not work in other states.

This raises a fundamental question: How strict should the pandemic policies have been?

In this chapter, I will formally introduce my idea of optimal stringency—a framework for determining the level of intervention that saves as many lives as possible while avoiding the unnecessary social, economic, and educational harms that extreme measures can produce.

Figure 3.3 summarizes this idea in the simplest form with two variables. The vertical axis represents "net social benefits," a measure that combines the positive effects of intervention (such as reducing cases and deaths, preserving hospital capacity, and protecting high-risk populations etc.) minus the social and economic costs (including learning loss, reduced GDP and production, and broader disruptions to daily life). The horizontal axis shows the stringency of the NPIs, ranging from school closures, to stay-at-home orders and bans on public gatherings.

While early interventions were essential to slow the initial spread of the virus, the relationship between stringency and overall welfare is not linear. At low levels, increasing stringency raises net social benefits: positive effects, such as reduced infection and fewer deaths, grow faster than the associated economic and social costs.

However, beyond a certain level, this relationship reverses. Additional restrictions continue to yield some epidemiological benefits, but the marginal costs, learning loss, reduced GDP and productivity, mental strain, and social disruption grow faster than the marginal gains. As a result, net social benefits begin to decline.

Figure 3.3 depicts this logic. The curve peaks at an optimal level of stringency, where the benefits of intervention and the costs imposed on society are best balanced. Beyond this point, stricter NPIs may still reduce infections, but they are not efficient.

I argue that the global average level of stringency during COVID-19 was well to the right of this optimal point. In other words, this same exact level of benefit would have been reached by lower stringency, which is depicted by point A.

This is what I call excessive caution—the point where much of the world drifted beyond reason into paralysis. This state of "Global Average," shown in Fig. 3.3, reflects policies that prioritize safety over the benefits of society. It would be good to remember what Benjamin Franklin once said on this matter: "Those who would give up essential liberty, to purchase a little temporary safety, deserve neither liberty nor safety."

What began as a necessary emergency measure turned into overprotection, costing children's futures. Education, more than any other sector, bore the weight of this excessive inertia. The world tried to save lives; in doing so, however, we risked the education of an entire generation.

As we look ahead, the lesson is clear. The next crisis will demand a balance of safety and liberty. Only by finding that "optimal strategy," where health protection and social well-being meet, can we avoid repeating mistakes that turned a health emergency into an educational catastrophe.

This and similar findings, some of which are presented, for example, in the chapter "Educationally Yours," suggest that the issue was not the use of NPIs themselves, but rather their excessive stringency, which disrupted nearly all nations.

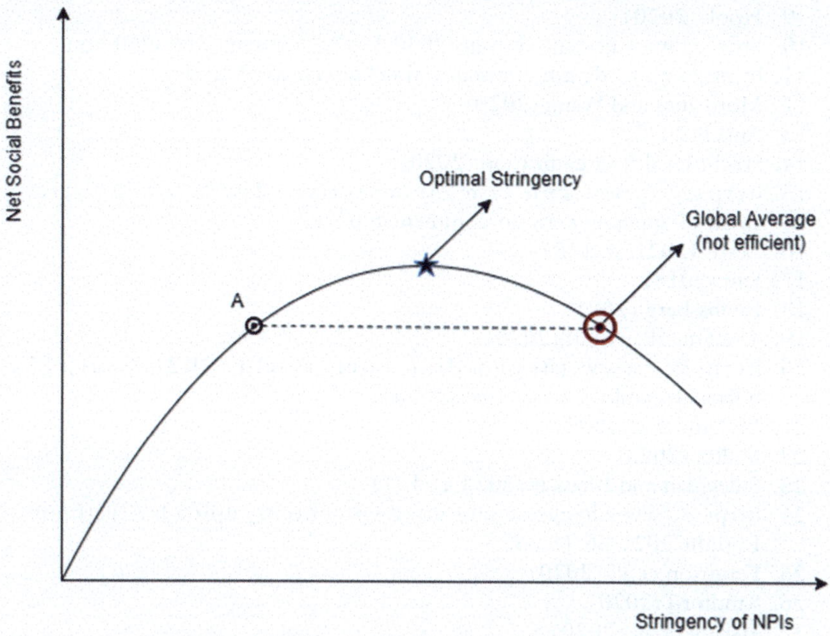

Fig. 3.3 The theory of stringency and net social benefits. Stringency reflects how strictly non-pharmaceutical interventions (NPIs) are implemented, while net benefits captures their broader impact—not only in preventing infections and deaths, but also in mitigating economic and social consequences. Net benefits considers Benefits minus costs, such as economic, social costs, mental health burdens, and disruptions to education

Notes

1. Yong (2018)
2. Spinney (2017, p. 171); Yong (2018)
3. National Intelligence Council (2004)
4. National Research Council (2016)
5. Cheng et al. (2007), Wong et al. (2019)
6. Global Preparedness Monitoring Board (2019)
7. Nuclear Threat Initiative (2019)
8. See, for example, Jones et al. (2008), Snowden (2019), World Health Organization (WHO) (2007)

9. Hook (2020)
10. https://www.gov.cn/xinwen/2020-11/25/content_5563960.htm
11. https://www.cdc.gov/museum/timeline/covid19.html
12. Moritsugu and Wang (2020)
13. Ankel (2020)
14. World Health Organization (2020)
15. https://www.cnn.com/interactive/2020/10/politics/covid-disappearing-trump-comment-tracker/
16. Lewis (2021, p. 163)
17. Sun (2018)
18. Kuenssberg (2021)
19. The Guardian Staff (2020)
20. https://www.theguardian.com/world/2020/mar/15/bolsonaro-amlo-coronavirus-warnings
21. McNutt et al. (2021)
22. Mallin (2023)
23. Suleyman and Bhaskar (2023, p. 177)
24. https://www.hsgac.senate.gov/wp-content/uploads/Testimony-Ebright-2024-06-18.pdf
25. Ferguson et al. (2020)
26. Sandford (2020)
27. Hsiang et al. (2020)
28. Davis et al. (2023)
29. By "state," the authors refer to the officials and legislatures of the 55 U.S. states, commonwealths, and territories, as well as the District of Columbia.
30. https://www.edweek.org/leadership/the-coronavirus-spring-the-historic-closing-of-u-s-schools-a-timeline/2020/07
31. https://ballotpedia.org/States_that_issued_lockdown_and_stay-at-home_orders_in_response_to_the_coronavirus_(COVID-19)_pandemic,_2020
32. Macedo and Lee (2025, p. 130)
33. The corresponding deaths per million were as follows: Italy: 463, Spain: 525, U.K.: 391, USA: 198.
34. https://www.theguardian.com/world/2020/jun/07/cuba-coronavirus-success-contact-tracing-isolation
35. It is, however, important to note that despite this early success, Cuba ultimately experienced one of the highest excess mortality rates later in the pandemic.
36. Kahl and Wright (2021, p. 163)
37. Global Preparedness Monitoring Board (2020)

38. Mathieu et al. (2020)
39. Tooze (2024)
40. Foster et al. (2024)
41. Hill and Artiga (2022); Tai et al. (2022)
42. Mendoza Cardozo et al. (2023)
43. McGowan and Bambra (2022)
44. Cervia-Hasler et al. (2024)
45. Mukherjee et al. (2022)
46. https://www.nytimes.com/2023/02/21/opinion/do-mask-mandates-work.html
47. https://www.nytimes.com/2023/03/10/opinion/masks-work-cochrane-study.html
48. Aiello et al. (2012); Lyu and Wehby (2020); Prakash et al. (2022) support the usage of masks combined with other hygiene methods. In a randomized trial, Aiello et al. (2012) found that combining masks with hand hygiene significantly reduced influenza-like illness among university students, while masks alone showed no clear effect. Lyu and Wehby (2020) reported that state mask mandates were followed by reductions in COVID-19 case growth, potentially averting hundreds of thousands of cases, but the estimates rely on intent-to-treat effects without compliance data and cannot fully rule out other simultaneous behavioral or policy changes.

    The research Jefferson et al. (2023) offers more skeptical conclusion.
49. https://www.nytimes.com/2020/03/24/business/economy/coronavirus-economy.html
50. Brusselaers et al. (2022)
51. https://cepr.org/voxeu/columns/swedens-constitution-decides-its-exceptional-covid-19-policy
52. Brusselaers et al. (2022)
53. https://www.aftonbladet.se/nyheter/a/xPvX6j/professorernas-rad-testa-att-stanga-skolor
54. Henley (2020); Irwin (2020)
55. https://www.svd.se/a/xPvvlX/presstraff-i-dag-med-utbildningsministern
56. https://omni.se/en-hel-generation-haller-pa-att-forlora-sin-framtid/a/AdMo9q
57. https://www.telegraph.co.uk/travel/ski/news/sweden-ski-resorts-remain-open-despite-coronavirus-spread/
58. https://www.expressen.se/kronikorer/viktor-barth-kron/regeringen-spelar-hogt-det-kan-sluta-i-fiasko/
59. Anderberg (2022, p. 92)
60. Giesecke (2020)

61. Anderberg (2022, p. 106)
62. Anderberg (2022, p. 224)
63. Erdbrink (2020)
64. See Alwan et al. (2020); Brusselaers et al. (2022); Pierre (2020), though the paper by Alwan et al. (2020) is more of a policy statement than original empirical research.
65. Markel et al. (2007)
66. Hatchett et al. (2007)
67. https://www.statnews.com/2020/06/19/faster-response-prevented-most-us-covid-19-deaths/
68. Hale et al. (2021)
69. Haerpfer et al. (2022)
70. Kahl and Wright (2021, p. 219)
71. https://www.yahoo.com/news/peru-locked-down-hard-early-174039274.html
72. Definition is here: https://www.economist.com/graphic-detail/2021/05/13/how-we-estimated-the-true-death-toll-of-the-pandemic, data is here: https://github.com/owid/covid-19-data/blob/master/public/data/excess_mortality/excess_mortality_economist_estimates.csv
73. A negative figure indicates that Greenland had fewer deaths by the end of 2022 than its historical average.
74. Pizzato et al. (2024)
75. https://iris.who.int/server/api/core/bitstreams/ae899862-9a24-4406-96c7-6a2e07eeb36a/content
76. https://youtu.be/OwfQy1-qya8
77. https://thehill.com/opinion/healthcare/494034-the-data-are-in-stop-the-panic-and-end-the-total-isolation/
78. https://www.ons.gov.uk/aboutus/transparencyandgovernance/freedomofinformationfoi/averageageofthosewhohaddiedwithcovid19
79. https://catholicinsight.com/2020/04/03/an-open-letter-from-a-microbiologist-on-covid-19/
80. https://apnews.com/general-news-4f0b6285a57c8b2929e2aceb864e7675
81. Demirgüç-Kunt et al. (2021)
82. Bendavid et al. (2021)
83. https://www.1news.co.nz/2020/04/06/health-minister-apologises-to-public-after-a-clear-breach-of-covid-19-lockdown-rules/
84. https://www.theguardian.com/uk-news/2020/may/05/uk-coronavirus-adviser-prof-neil-ferguson-resigns-after-breaking-lockdown-rules

85. https://www.cnn.com/2020/03/16/politics/bill-de-blasio-gym-coronavirus
86. https://www.independent.co.uk/news/health/coronavirus-cancer-cases-covid-services-uk-macmillan-b1398672.html
87. https://www.connexionfrance.com/news/30000-cancer-cases-undetected-in-france-due-to-covid-19/446185

CHAPTER 4

Vaccinated

Abstract This chapter examines the rapid development and deployment of COVID-19 vaccines, highlighting both the scientific triumph and the uncertainties surrounding their effectiveness and long-term impact. It explores the role of mRNA technology and the global race for vaccination, while also addressing questions about distribution, equity, and real-world effectiveness. The chapter evaluates whether vaccines alone were sufficient to control the pandemic and situates them within the broader policy response.

Keywords Vaccines • Immunization • COVID-19 • Public health • Effectiveness • Distribution

Messieurs, c'est les microbes qui auront le dernier mot.(Gentlemen, it is the microbes who will have the last word.)
—Louis Pasteur

After the loss of funding for the Biological Research Center (BRC), where she had been working, 30-year-old Dr. Karikó made the difficult decision to leave her native Hungary, where she spent her entire life.[1] She had had very bad days and struggles in Hungary, but had never contemplated leaving it until that day. Her father was persecuted by the Hungarian government, vilified, and sacked, having become a political pariah. Her name was

O. Erdem, *The Socioeconomic Impact of Pandemics*,
https://doi.org/10.1007/978-3-032-24189-4_4

removed from the Study Award, the most prestigious student merit award for college students, even though she had originally been on the list. She was also threatened by the secret police. At that point, realizing that the only way to pursue her scientific aspirations was to move to a country where science and scientists were more appreciated, she evaluated a couple of labs in Britain, along with institutions in Spain, France, and the United States, before finally deciding to apply to institutions in "America." This was in the year 1985. She decided to relocate temporarily after accepting an invitation from Dr. Suhadolnik at Temple University in Philadelphia, Pennsylvania to take up a post with an annual salary of $17,000. At this point, she was planning to return to her native Hungary. However, even a temporary relocation required some money, which she lacked. At that time, most Eastern European countries were implementing capital controls, which restricted the amount of money citizens could take abroad. The Hungarian government had set that amount at $50. Dr. Karikó sold her car, exchanged the proceeds for £900, equivalent to about $1200, and concealed the money inside the teddy bear of her two-year-old daughter Susan (who would later become a two-time Olympic gold medalist in rowing). She then departed with her husband and daughter.[2]

Dr. Karikó worked at Dr. Suhadolnik's lab at Temple University, which she described as long-neglected and "filthy," finding it infested with cockroaches. Despite these conditions, she remained diligent, publishing numerous papers, including three in a single issue of *Biochemistry*, a respected peer-reviewed academic journal.

In 1988, she received a job offer from Johns Hopkins University, an opportunity that could have been the defining moment of her career. This was a chance to work at one of the world's top medical institutions. She kept the offer secret from her advisor and employer, Dr. Suhadolnik, unaware of the power he held over her immigration status.

When Dr. Suhadolnik learned of her decision, he was stunned. He gave her an ultimatum: stay in his lab or return to Hungary. He removed her name from several research papers that were in the pre-publication stage. Taking matters further, he contacted Johns Hopkins to block her employment, citing visa restrictions. He also reported her to Immigration Services, leading to an inquiry into potential visa violations.

With no path forward at Johns Hopkins, and unable to remain in Dr. Suhadolnik's lab in the face of his relentless fury, she faced an uncertain future. However, with the support of other scientists, she secured a doctoral fellowship at the Uniformed Services University of the Health

Sciences, a military medical school, located in a different state. Leaving Pennsylvania behind, she relocated and threw herself into her work, often sleeping in the lab as she tirelessly pursued her research. Soon, in 1989, she joined the University of Pennsylvania (UPenn) as an assistant professor, where she worked for six years experimenting with messenger RNA (mRNA). As later remarked by Dr. Anthony Fauci, director of the National Institutes of Allergy and Infectious Diseases, "She was, in a positive sense, kind of obsessed with the concept of messenger RNA."[3]

Discovered in 1960, mRNA molecules instruct cells to produce specific proteins. Later research was focused on injecting mRNA into cells to direct them to fight diseases. In 1978, scientists delivered mRNA in liposomes into mouse and human cells, prompting them to produce the encoded protein. This breakthrough showed mRNA's potential for directing protein synthesis. Liposomes, tiny vesicles, protected the fragile mRNA, thereby improving its stability. This early experiment paved the way for mRNA-based therapeutics, including vaccines and gene therapies.

Driven by this potential, she explored ways to program mRNA to harness the body's natural protein-production machinery for treating diseases and preventing infections, an approach now known as "RNA Therapeutics." She stated, "We could instruct the body to make specific proteins on demand.... The process would involve only temporary molecules that would then be easily degraded by ordinary cells."[4] Dr. Karikó likened this to a "manned spaceflight."

Most research universities require their faculty to secure grants to fund their labs, a system that places immense pressure on scientists to align their work with topics deemed fundable or immediately impactful. During her time at UPenn, Dr. Karikó faced significant challenges in securing financial support for her groundbreaking ideas about mRNA. Despite her persistence and numerous grant proposals, both federal and private funding bodies rejected her work, considering it too unconventional. Her ideas failed to gain traction with funders or institutional decision-makers, leaving her research largely unsupported. In her words, she "never got a dime" for her mRNA projects. Driven by a pure desire to pursue science for its own sake, she found herself at odds with a system that demanded she market her ideas to attract funding, something she struggled to do. The consequences were severe: she was discouraged from attending departmental and grant meetings, students were reportedly told not to collaborate with her, and she was even denied access to shared lab materials. The environment grew increasingly hostile, isolating her from the very community she sought to contribute to.

Amid these challenges, in January 1995 she also underwent a lumpectomy—a procedure to remove a tumor from her breast. Balancing the demands of her groundbreaking but unfunded research with her health struggles, she pressed on, undeterred by the setbacks.

The challenges did not stop there. In February 1995, the University of Pennsylvania's tenure committee removed her from the tenure track, a career-altering decision that not only represented a professional setback but also led to her demotion. For many academics, such a blow would mark the end of their research careers, but Dr. Karikó's response was one of extraordinary resilience. "When I am knocked down, I know how to pick myself up," she told to *The Telegraph*, reflecting her determination to science.[5]

Refusing to abandon her vision, Dr. Karikó chose to remain at UPenn as a non-tenure-track professor. Her title was "senior research investigator" (instead of associate professor). Without the job security or prestige that tenure affords, she continued to work tirelessly on mRNA research, driven not by recognition or financial reward but by her belief in the potential of mRNA to revolutionize medicine. This decision required remarkable courage and sacrifice, as non-tenure-track positions often come with fewer resources, less institutional support, and limited opportunities for advancement.

One day, in 1997, by the photocopy machine at UPenn, she met Drew Weissman, a newly appointed MD/PHD immunologist at UPenn and soon-to-be her lifelong collaborator. During their small talk, Dr. Weissman mentioned that he had been working on an HIV vaccine. Excited by the possibility of collaboration, she offered him a potential solution: mRNA. He was an immunologist with little knowledge of mRNAs, and she was a molecular biologist unfamiliar with immunology. That chance encounter marked the beginning of a lifelong scientific collaboration and friendship. He was intrigued by her expertise and enthusiasm for creating therapeutic approaches using mRNA. Together, they began working on developing an HIV vaccine using mRNA. It was pure luck.

However, when the mRNAs were injected into mice, the animals' cells produced the desired proteins, but there was a catch: they also triggered infections, potentially leading to severe symptoms or even death. This outcome deeply disappointed Dr. Karikó, more than any other challenge she had faced in her lifetime. She was at a crossroads: abandon the field or uncover the cause of the problem. She chose the latter.

Together with Dr. Drew Weissman, over the years she conducted hundreds, if not thousands, of experiments to understand why mRNAs provoked inflammation. They eventually hypothesized that the immune system was reacting to certain chemical features of the synthetic RNA. To solve this, they modified the nucleosides—the building blocks of RNA—replacing uridine with pseudouridine to make the mRNA less detectable by the immune system and reduce inflammatory responses.

Despite their innovative approach, many prestigious journals, including *Science* and *Nature*, rejected their idea. In 2005, they published their paper on Immunity, but it failed to receive much attention.[6] The paper was cited 948 times in the 15 years between its publication in 2005 and 2019, before the onset of COVID-19 It then received almost 2000 citations in the five years following the emergence of COVID-19.

Believing in the potential of their discovery, Karikó and Weissman co-founded a company called RNARx. They were convinced the breakthrough would spark such widespread interest that their phone would never stop ringing. For years, however, the silence persisted. They received only two invitations to present their work—one from a conference in Japan, the other in New York City. They also reached out to investors, but neither the investment community nor academic institutions showed interest in funding her research, dismissing mRNA therapy as a dead end.

Dr. Karikó stayed at UPenn until 2013, the year when she realized, after returning from a conference in Japan, that she was no longer valued by the university.[7] Despite the groundbreaking nature of her research, the scientific community had yet to recognize its significance. The department chair informed her that the university had hired a new faculty member in her place, citing her failure to secure major grants or publish in top-tier journals. They offered her a cramped workspace near the animal facility if she chose to stay.

She had endured enough and decided to retire, keeping an adjunct title. As she walked away, she delivered a quiet, but prophetic remark: "One day, this lab is going to be a museum." Looking back later, she would summarize the moment more bluntly: "I was kicked out of UPenn and was forced to retire."[8] The department chair paid little attention. Still, she and Dr. Weissman continued their relentless pursuit of mRNA-based vaccines. Dr. Karikó began searching for opportunities outside the university—places that had already recognized the potential of mRNA technology.

Dr. Karikó's daughter, an Olympic rower, won gold medals at both the 2008 and 2012 Olympics. While attending one of her daughter's games in Europe, Dr. Karikó met the husband-and-wife team of, Uğur Şahin and Özlem Türeci, Turkish-born physicians and co-founders of the biotechnology company BioNTech, in Germany. At the time, they were pioneering personalized cancer therapies, moving away from the conventional one-size-fits-all approaches like radiation, surgery, and chemotherapy. Their warm conversation and interest in mRNA resulted in Dr. Şahin extending her an offer for the vice president position at BioNTech.

Ironically, when she shared her decision to join BioNTech with her peers and administrators, they laughed at her, remarking "BioNTech doesn't even have a website."[9] In 2014, Dr. Karikó joined BioNTech, to work on a cancer vaccine using mRNA technology. Together with Drs. Şahin and Özlem Türeci, she published many papers on cancer.

Meanwhile, another group of scientists, again including Dr. Karikó, showed that chemically modified mRNA wrapped in lipid nanoparticles could safely and effectively protect mice and monkeys from the Zika virus, laying the groundwork for mRNA vaccines like those used for COVID-19.[10] This approach involves packaging the mRNA molecules in small fat-like particles, which helps prevent the mRNA from being detected and destroyed by the body's immune system. By using these particles as cargo vehicles, the mRNA can be safely delivered into cells, where it can be released to instruct the cell to produce the specific proteins needed for a curative or vaccine response. Dr. Karikó and Dr. Weissman adopted this idea for their mRNA studies.

BioNTech went public on the NASDAQ in October 2019, raising $150 million (with a market value of $3.4 billion), just two months before the onset of the COVID-19 pandemic.

First Vaccine

COVID-19 hit the world at the end of 2019; at that time, no one would have predicted the pandemic would be so devastating. By the end of February 2020, just three months after the start of the outbreak, 3000 people had lost their lives to the virus. Expectations for a vaccine were cautious at best. Most experts estimated that development would take several years. In February, Antoni Fauci, who was then the director of the National Institute of Allergy and Infectious Diseases at the National

Institutes of Health (NIAID) and public spokesperson about the pandemic, stated:

> It means you have taken the first step towards the vaccine, which by anybody's calculation is going to be at least a year to a year and a half at best, and that is if we proceed under the emergency authorization of the regulatory agencies.[11]

What most of the scientists agreed on at that time was that the world needed not only the latest tools of science and scientific thinking but also luck. Both the American pharmaceutical company Moderna and the German biotechnology company BioNTech were interested in exploring the idea of mRNA vaccines that Dr. Karikó and her team had been working on for years. However, they needed the genetic sequence of the virus. On January 11, 2020, Chinese researcher Zhang Yongzhen granted permission to Australian virologist Edward C. Holmes to share the 30,000-letter genetic sequence of the virus with the international scientific community.,[1213] Using machine learning tools, Moderna completed the mRNA COVID-19 vaccine sequence—a process that traditionally takes months—in just two days, marking a significant leap in rapid vaccine development.[14] BioNTech collaborated with the American company Pfizer, initially without even a formal written contract.[15] By February 24, 2020, they had completed the initial formulation of their COVID-19 vaccine. Just weeks later, on March 16, the first dose was administered to a clinical trial participant. Rigorous clinical testing continued throughout the year, culminating in a major announcement in November: Pfizer and BioNTech announced that their vaccine was 91% effective,[16] setting a record for the fastest vaccine development.

On December 8, 2020, Margaret Keenan, a 90-year-old grandma, rolled up her sleeve and became the first person in the world to receive Pfizer's authorized COVID-19 vaccine. The first thing she said was: "I can finally look forward to spending time with my family and friends in the new year after being on my own for most of the year."[17] She became so famous that sales of the penguin T-shirt she wore, given to her by the hospital, soared all around the world after she received the jab.

Later that year, other companies declared even higher rates of efficacy. Chinese researchers introduced their vaccines, too. While most of the world favored Western companies such as Pfizer &BioNTech, Moderna, and AstraZeneca, countries such as Türkiye (Turkey), Indonesia, and Brazil opted to receive vaccines from China's Sinovac.

In 2023, Katalin Karikó, now a professor at Szeged University in Hungary, received the Nobel Prize in Physiology or Medicine. She chronicled her journey in the memoir *Breaking Through*, a book that has been invaluable to me—not only in writing this one, but also on a personal level.

While her story offers a wealth of lessons—perseverance, resilience, the power of belief in science, and the importance of hard work—this book will primarily focus on one key aspect: the transformative impact of her work on vaccine development. The fastest vaccine development in history did not happen overnight. It was a story of sweat, disappointment, and hard work. By a measure, it had been explored for its potential application in vaccines for three decades before its successful creation.[18] COVID-19 prompted the acceleration of the mRNA vaccines. The ideas of Katalin Karikó and Drew Weissman formed the basis for the COVID-19 vaccines, which saved millions of lives in 2020 and 2021.

According to Our World in Data, as of November 2023, 70.5% of the global population has received at least one dose of a COVID-19 vaccine, and a total of 13.51 billion doses have been administered worldwide. Approximately 5.6 billion people received at least one dose in the three years between 2020 and 2023. This marks an unprecedented scale of vaccination within such a brief period in human history. For comparison, it took almost 32 years for scientists to create, develop, and implement the first malaria vaccine, Mosquirix.[19] An analysis of all vaccines developed in the history of mankind, excluding smallpox[20] and COVID-19, reveals that the average time from microbe identification to vaccine development was 48 years. Furthermore, it took an average of 53 years to reach a global vaccination coverage of 75%.[21] Humanity was fortunate that Dr. Karikó and her collaborators did not give up on their work for science and society, long before COVID-19 even emerged.

However, the distribution of the vaccine across nations was not equal. While almost 80% of the population in high-income countries has received at least one vaccine dose, the figure drops to 33% in low-income countries.,[22,23]

Within nations, some countries lacked clear equity-based criteria for prioritizing vaccines. For example, many African countries' COVID-19 plans created conditions in which allocation could be inconsistent or vulnerable to influence. Few plans put forward explicit criteria for deciding which groups should be prioritized.[24] Most other countries established priority rankings to determine which groups were to receive vaccinations first.[25] This approach was broadly justified, considering that certain groups, such as the elderly and first-responders, faced higher risks of infection and severe outcomes. However, in several countries, such as those in Türkiye and Philippines, reports suggested that these priority systems were sometimes manipulated to favor already advantaged groups or serve electoral considerations.[26] For example, Türkiye's early vaccine rollout and vaccination framework included a category labeled "people in critical jobs," without clearly specifying which occupations were qualified under this category. This ambiguity drew sharp criticism from everybody, including members of the Turkish parliament.[27] Some members of the opposition party questioned whether the category was being used to include individuals with close ties to the governing party.[28]

Did Vaccines Save Us?

Humanity was not very lucky when the Spanish flu hit the world in 1918. Technology and science were not as developed as they are today. As a result, no vaccine was produced, and the pandemic claimed an estimated 50 to 100 million lives worldwide.

The total number of excess deaths attributed to COVID-19 is estimated at 7 million, roughly 0.8% of the global population. While non-pharmaceutical interventions (NPIs), such as social distancing and mask mandates, were successfully implemented in many parts of the world during the 1918 Spanish flu, vaccines were not available then due to the limited state of medical science. In contrast, vaccines proved to be the defining difference between the two pandemics. An analysis of 185 countries and territories by researchers at Imperial College London estimated that COVID-19 vaccines saved approximately 14 million lives in 2021 alone.[29] According to *The Economist*, nearly 12 million of these lives were saved by just two vaccines: AstraZeneca-Oxford and Pfizer-BioNTech.[30] Vaccines significantly reduced the severity of infections, easing pressure on overwhelmed hospitals and enabling healthcare systems to continue essential services. They also allowed economies to reopen safely, helping restore workforce participation and revive critical sectors like travel, hospitality, and education. While vaccines did not eliminate COVID-19, they transformed a deadly pandemic into a manageable public health challenge and were central to the world's recovery. Vaccines made the difference. They saved lives.

Notes

1. Karikó (2023, p. 130)
2. Karikó (2023, p. 138)
3. Kolata (2021)
4. Karikó (2023, p. 168)
5. Newey and Nuki (2020)
6. Karikó et al. (2005)
7. Miller Joe et al. (2022)
8. https://www.youtube.com/watch?v=514nzDeT7WM
9. https://www.wired.com/story/mrna-coronavirus-vaccine-pfizer-biontech/
10. Pardi et al. (2017)
11. https://abcnews.go.com/Health/health-experts-warn-life-saving-coronavirus-vaccine-years/story?id=69032902
12. Bradsher (2024)
13. Holmes (2020)
14. https://aws.amazon.com/solutions/case-studies/moderna-machine-learning/
15. https://scrip.citeline.com/SC144598/How-Pfizer-Crafted-Its-Own-Operation-Warp-Speed-For-The-COVID-19-Vaccine
16. https://www.statnews.com/2020/11/09/covid-19-vaccine-from-pfizer-and-biontech-is-strongly-effective-early-data-from-large-trial-indicate/
17. https://www.theguardian.com/world/2020/dec/08/coventry-woman-90-first-patient-to-receive-covid-vaccine-in-nhs-campaign
18. Pecetta et al. (2022)
19. Laurens (2020)
20. Smallpox was the only disease for which a vaccine was developed before the microbe was identified. Despite this, it claimed the lives of between 300 million and 500 million people in the twentieth century.
21. Glassman et al. (2022)
22. https://ourworldindata.org/covid-vaccinations
23. *United Nations Development Programme (UNDP), Global Dashboard for Vaccine Equity* (n.d.)
24. Kapiriri et al. (2022)
25. Turkiye: https://www.milliyet.com.tr/gundem/son-dakika-koronavirus-asisinda-oncelik-listesi-guncellendi-6405788, United Kingdom: https://www.gov.uk/government/publications/priority-groups-for-coronavirus-covid-19-vaccination-advice-from-the-jcvi-2-december-2020/priority-groups-for-

coronavirus-covid-19-vaccination-advice-from-the-jcvi-2-december-2020, France: https://en.wikipedia.org/wiki/COVID-19_vaccination_in_France
26. Sirin (2021) and https://www.scmp.com/news/asia/southeast-asia/article/3126976/coronavirus-philippine-mayors-accused-vaccine-queue
27. https://www.birgun.net/haber/covid-19-asisinda-torpil-donemi-331470
28. https://www.sozcu.com.tr/corona-asisinda-torpil-iddiasi-wp6235173
29. Watson et al. (2022)
30. The Economist (2022)

CHAPTER 5

Masks, Vaccines, and the Crisis of Faith in Science

Abstract This chapter explores the erosion of public trust in science and institutions during the pandemic. It analyzes how conflicting messages, politicization of health measures, and misinformation contributed to skepticism toward masks, vaccines, and expert guidance. The chapter argues that the pandemic exposed a deeper crisis of credibility in modern societies, where scientific authority is increasingly contested, complicating effective public health responses.

Keywords Trust in science • Misinformation • Masks • Vaccines • Polarization • Public perception

One of the stark realities of COVID-19 was the deep divide over medical practices, not only regarding non-pharmaceutical interventions (NPIs) but also vaccines. Scientists, journalists, and the public were sharply split not only on the effectiveness of these measures but also on their necessity. This polarization stemmed from a complex interplay of political, historical, and psychological factors.

Lasting for 40 years, from 1932 to 1972, "The Tuskegee Study of Untreated Syphilis in the Negro Male" was one of the longest scientific experiments ever conducted.[1] The purpose of the research was to observe the development and damage of syphilis. Researchers from the U.S. Public Health Service, working with Tuskegee Institute—a historically Black college in Alabama—recruited more than 600 African American men aged 25

O. Erdem, *The Socioeconomic Impact of Pandemics*,
https://doi.org/10.1007/978-3-032-24189-4_5

and older to participate in the study.[2] The subjects were informed that they would receive free medical care, free meals, and burial insurance[3] and were told that they would be treated for "bad blood," a general term that was used to mean anemia, fatigue, and syphilis. Convinced they had joined a benevolent health program, they placed their trust in the study's organizers. Unbeknownst to them, roughly 200 participants were given placebos instead of any therapeutic agent. Even after penicillin was discovered as a treatment for syphilis in 1947, the researchers deliberately withheld it, allowing the disease to advance unchecked.

Over the course of the study, 7 men are estimated to have died directly because of the illness, and 154 because of heart disease, as a consequence of being untreated.[4] This is particularly shocking, considering that a treatment *was* available. In 1972, journalist Jean Heller revealed the immorality of the experiment, leading to its discontinuation.[5] A federal lawsuit ensued, resulting in a $10 million settlement. Additionally, President Bill Clinton formally apologized to the victims.[6]

Jean Heller later received various journalism accolades, one of which was the Raymond Clapper Memorial Award. Remarkably, the journalists who broke the Watergate Scandal were awarded second place in the Clapper Awards. The Tuskegee Study is routinely cited, especially in Black communities, as a reason to doubt government-led health initiatives, offering an illustration of how historical injustices can erode public trust and, decades later, shape vaccination decisions worldwide. These echoes persist. Even in 2020, for example, surveys in Gambia found that 70% of adults preferred prayer to vaccines.[7]

The legacy of the Tuskegee study continues to resonate today. Drawing on survey responses from nearly 120,000 adults in 113 countries, researchers from the UK, Brazil, and Bangladesh showed an inverse link between trust in government and COVID-19 vaccine hesitancy. In other words, the lower the level of trust in government, the higher the vaccine hesitance. Each one-step increase on a four-point trust scale boosts predicted vaccine uptake by about six percentage points, from roughly 54% among those who "trust not at all" to 71% among those who "trust a lot" (see Fig. 5.1).[8]

What drives the lack of trust? Several factors can be cited: political beliefs, age, and education.

Let's start with political beliefs, or partisanship, where people are prone to adhere to the implicit rules of their societies, even when they might not agree with them. This is an effect which was shown years ago by a couple,

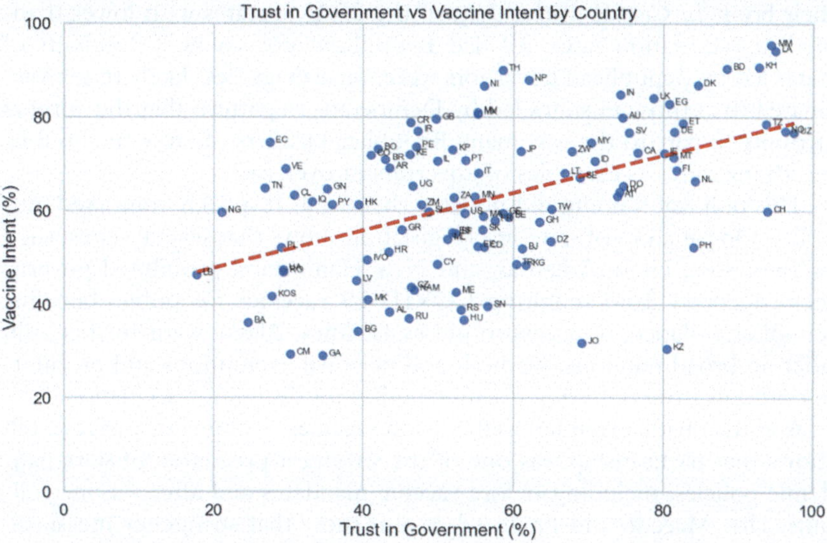

Fig. 5.1 Trust in government vs. vaccine intent by country. There is an inverse relationship between vaccine hesitancy and trust in government. (Source: Prepared by the author, using Wellcome Global Monitor Wave 2 (2020) Full Public Dataset at https://wellcome.org/reports/wellcome-global-monitor-covid-19/2020#downloads-6b45)

Muzafer Sherif and Carolyn Sherif, who are acknowledged as the founders of modern social psychology.[9] They devised an experiment in the 1950s, where children were taken to a camp and asked to list their best friends after they spent some time with their peers. The researchers then divided the children into two groups—Red Devils and Bull Dogs—without imposing any functional relationship, competition, or rivalry between the groups. Each child was simply in one of these two groups. The researchers then asked the same question: List the names of your best friends in the camp. The kids predominantly chose their best friends from their own group. The list of Red Devil kids consisted of 95% of children from their group (compared with an initial figure of 35%), while the list of Bull Dogs included 88% from their own group (again initially 35%). This research highlighted the group adherence behavior, a phenomenon that still remains relevant today, especially during the COVID-19 pandemic. Princeton University professors Stephen Macedo and Frances Lee show, in their book *In Covid's Wake*, that, of the 25 U.S. states with lower-than-median vaccination rates, 19 had Republican governors.[10] Residents of states led by Republican governors were, on average, less likely to get vaccinated than those in states led by Democrats—a pattern that the authors attribute in part to the way many Republican leaders often framed public health measures as examples of government overreach.

This political framing did not stay rhetorical. It quickly translated into policy. One analysis of state-level legislation shows that several states, such as Tennessee, Utah, Arkansas, and New Hampshire, prohibited government agencies from requiring COVID-19 vaccines for public benefits, school attendance, or access to public facilities. Alaska went further still, offering broad religious, medical, and personal exemptions and prohibiting officials from requiring documentation for declining vaccination.

And the divide extended well beyond vaccines. A large body of research shows that partisanship was one of the strongest predictors of state pandemic policies, including before vaccine mandates and after vaccine rollouts. Drs. Macedo and Frances Lee also show that stringency measures, including school closures and reopenings, were strongly correlated with the political leanings of different regions. On average, Republican-led states adopted fewer stringency measures, whereas Democratic-led states implemented stricter ones.[11]

In one recent study, researchers surveyed 3000 Americans to understand the reasons for the variance in their health-related behavior during the pandemic. They revealed that "partisanship was the best predictor of differences in behaviors, attitudes, and preferences than anything else that we measure."[12] In other words, people's health practices, like mask-wearing and vaccination, were mostly shaped by their party affiliation. Republicans were less likely to wear masks and get vaccinated, a behavior, overridden by influences from news consumption, local policies, or pandemic-related deaths. Group adherence has been shaping people's decisions for centuries. According to the Kaiser Family Foundation (KFF)'s COVID-19 Vaccine Monitor, 91% of Democrats have received at least one dose. In stark contrast, uptake falls to 66% among Republicans.[13]

The stark differences between the two political parties in the U.S. raise an ultimate question: Which vaccine behavior was the most effective or was associated with the lowest death rates across society?

A 2023 study by researchers at Yale analyzed over 538,000 deaths among adults in Florida and Ohio. They found that excess mortality was similar across parties before vaccines were widely available to all adults in

April 2021. However, after that date, the excess mortality was significantly higher among Republican voters than Democrats. After April 2021, the mortality gap widened to 7.7 percentage points, with Republicans experiencing a 43% higher excess death rate, particularly in counties with low vaccination rates.[14] Although vaccine hesitancy exists across political lines, the scale of politicization in the U.S. far exceeds that in other developed nations.[15] So, according to this research, the effects of NPIs did not differ substantially across states with different political tendencies, but the pattern shifted after the vaccine rollout, to which Republicans were more hesitant.

Certainly, lack of trust is not the sole reason behind people's vaccine hesitancy. There is a psychological effect of rumors, conspiracies, and urban legends, too. For exampl, during the 1831–1832 cholera outbreak in Britain, particularly in Liverpool, riots erupted due to a widespread belief that doctors were deliberately killing cholera patients to use their bodies for anatomical dissection. This fear was fueled by earlier scandals involving grave robbing and body snatching, including the infamous Burke and Hare case in Edinburgh just four years earlier, in which two men murdered victims and sold their bodies to a local anatomy school. In Liverpool, public anger boiled over, with rioters reportedly shouting, "Bring out the Burkers!"—a chilling echo of those earlier crimes. It's a fascinating look at how public mistrust of medicine and social tensions collided during a health crisis (Fig. 5.2).[16]

Chip Heath and his co-authors from Duke University presented various scenarios to Duke University undergraduate students to see which stories were more likely to be spread. Consider these two scenarios and decide which one is more disgusting:

1. There was a bird imbedded in the grill of Mike's car.
2. There was an 8-year-old girl imbedded in the grill of Mike's car.

Or this one:

1. The waiter had told the chef to prepare the dog for dinner. The couple ran into the kitchen to save poor Rosa just in time.
2. The couple enjoyed their delicious meal. They eventually realized that the waiter had served them Rosa for dinner.

Fig. 5.2 Police incident during the 1885 smallpox epidemic in Montreal. Source: Drawn by Robert Harris (1849–1919). The illustration was initially published on page 781 in November 28, 1885, edition of *Harper's Weekly*, as a supplement to an article called "The Pestilence in Montreal." Public domain via Wikimedia Commons. https://commons.wikimedia.org/wiki/File:An_incident_of_the_smallpox_epidemics_in_Montreal.jpg

In both scenarios, the version in (ii) is deliberately designed to evoke stronger disgust. When people were asked which scenario they would pass along more, they mostly picked (ii), the version that produced a higher level of disgust. The authors concluded that "emotion rather than truth may sometimes win out in the marketplace of ideas." A story grounded in truth but enhanced, even exaggerated, with heightened emotion has a greater chance of spreading.

This tendency helps explain what happens during any crisis, including the COVID-19 pandemic. In a moment of uncertainty and fear, stories that triggered strong emotions, especially disgust, tend to travel faster.

Rumors that vaccines were quickly developed, implying they might not be safe, that they could alter one's DNA, that they would make individuals infertile, or that they contained microchips for controlling humanity, circulated widely all around the world. False news not only has a higher probability of being propagated but also spreads to more people at a faster rate. This is what three Massachusetts Institute of Technology (MIT) professors showed in their study. Examining 126,000 stories shared on Twitter (X) by approximately 3 million users, they published their results in the prestigious journal *Science*. Getting support from fact-checking organizations, they showed that the top 1% of false news reaches between 1000 and 100,000 people, while the truth seldom spreads to over 1000 individuals. Moreover, they also showed that the truth took approximately six times longer than falsehood to reach 1500 people.[17] Therefore, any false news concerning vaccines was far more likely to be disseminated to a larger population, further influencing some people's hesitancy to receive vaccinations.

The bottom line is that vaccine science is far more complex than most laypeople can readily grasp. People often fear what they do not understand; in that vacuum, misinformation flourishes. Those who do understand the science, therefore, have a responsibility to communicate it clearly and completely. Moreover, science should serve as a tool to help and empower people, not a weapon to dominate or silence. As Dr. Katalin Karikó notes, "Some of the fault may lie with those of us who understand the science but have failed to explain it fully." We still have a lot of work to do.

Notes

1. https://en.wikipedia.org/wiki/Tuskegee_Syphilis_Study
2. Breed (2022)
3. https://tools.cdc.gov/medialibrary/index.aspx#/media/id/281461
4. Breed (2022)
5. https://apnews.com/article/business-science-health-race-and-ethnicity-syphilis-e9dd07eaa4e74052878a68132cd3803a
6. https://clintonwhitehouse4.archives.gov/textonly/New/Remarks/Fri/19970516-898.html
7. https://unherd.com/2023/07/western-lockdowns-still-torment-africa/
8. Jennings et al. (2023)
9. Sherif and Sherif (1953)

10. Macedo and Lee (2025, p. 137)
11. Macedo and Lee (2025, p. 134)
12. Gadarian et al. (2021)
13. Sparks et al. (2023)
14. Wallace et al. (2023)
15. Burn-Murdoch (2022)
16. Burrell and Gill (2005)
17. Vosoughi et al. (2018)

PART III

Pandemically Yours

CHAPTER 6

Economically and Financially Yours

Abstract This chapter investigates the economic consequences of COVID-19, including declines in GDP, rising unemployment, inflation, and unprecedented government intervention. It highlights how stimulus policies reshaped monetary systems and contributed to long-term inflationary pressures. The chapter also emphasizes the unequal distribution of economic impacts, showing how poverty and inequality increased after decades of improvement, and analyzing the divergent effects on financial markets and asset prices.

Keywords Economic impact • Stimulus • Inequality • Inflation • Financial markets • Policy costs

One of my favorite pandemic stories, *The Plague* (original French title: *La Peste*), was written by the French author Albert Camus in 1947. Widely considered to be one of the most important works of the twentieth century, *The Plague* was one of the key works which contributed to Camus receiving the Nobel Prize in Literature a decade later.

The novel describes a fictional plague that takes place in the coastal Algerian city of Oran. It opens with the protagonist, Bernard Rieux, a dedicated doctor, noticing a dead rat in his building. That day, he pays little attention to it, kicking the rodent aside. Within days, rats begin

O. Erdem, *The Socioeconomic Impact of Pandemics*,
https://doi.org/10.1007/978-3-032-24189-4_6

appearing dead everywhere in the streets, basements, and buildings across the city. The situation then worsens, and the city's residents begin to fall ill. The first victim known to the doctor is Michel, the concierge in Rieux's own building.

Dr. Rieux identifies the disease as plague, but it takes him a long time to convince others. As Camus observes "There have been as many plagues as wars in history; yet always plagues and wars take people equally by surprise."[1] Initially, the authorities in Oran try to hide the outbreak and delay taking action until the death toll rises and the epidemic is undeniable. By this time the disease has become so severe and deadly that the citizens of Oran had nothing to do but think about survival.

Soon after, a quarantine is implemented, and the city gates are closed. The city is locked down and disconnected from the rest of the world. On a daily basis, newspapers publish new restrictions: about education, shopping, eating, and other aspects of social life. Restaurants put up notices stating that their utensils are sterilized. It is announced that attempts to leave the town will be punishable by imprisonment.

Vehicles and ships coming to Oran were turned away, shutting down the city's trade. The shortage of goods and services drives up prices, and it has become very difficult, if not impossible, to find the necessities. In spite of this situation, however, some people spend freely and recklessly. Instead of prioritizing essential goods, some have spent large sums of money on luxury items, perhaps to counteract the fear of plague.

In Camus's Oran, many businesses are shut down, and others operate at minimal capacity. Stores once thriving with trade now stand half-empty, as their supply lines collapse under quarantine. Cafés were closed, and the streets fell into idleness and silence. Merchants face ruin.

Material suffering with no medical remedy led the citizens of Oran to seek spiritual peace. Churches have started to offer weekly sermons, which attract large congregations. Father Paneloux, a Jesuit priest, suggests that the plague is God's punishment for their sin. Dr. Rieux, however, rejects this notion. To him, the plague is not a divine punishment but a human crisis, one that demanded action to save lives. Determined to fight against the plague, the doctor meets Tarrou, a visitor who has found himself trapped in Oran by the imposed restrictions. As their acquaintance grows, Dr. Rieux tells Tarrou, "All the same, when you see the misery it brings, you'd need to be a madman, or a coward, or stone blind, to give in tamely to the plague." Together with others, they decide to resist. Dr. Rieux, Tarrou, and Rambert have fought tirelessly. Tarrou has organized volunteer sanitary teams, and has worked side by side with Rieux, becoming his closest friend.

Months have passed, marked by deaths and the fear of dying. Eventually, however, the epidemic finally wanes and Oran celebrates its liberation. While the citizens rejoice, embracing one another in the streets and believing the nightmare to be over, Dr. Rieux tempers his optimism with caution. He has seen too much suffering to believe in easy victories. Camus closes the novel with a sober warning.

> He knew … that the plague bacillus never dies or disappears for good; that it can lie dormant for years and years … and that perhaps the day would come when, for the bane and enlightening of men, it would rouse up its rats again and send them forth to die in a happy city.[2]

If Camus taught us anything, it is that crises do not arrive equally, and that they do not impact people equally. The victims in his story were the concierges, the porters, and the people who lived in the basements. COVID-19 proved that lesson again.

Albert Camus was five years old when the Spanish flu hit the world in 1918. Though too young to remember how hard it was, he did grow up in its shadow. In French Algeria, where he was born and raised, he must have heard about the staggering mortality rates in nearby Spain and France, where fear and grief left deep scars. In his book *The Plague*, Camus offers not just a vivid picture of an epidemic through economic, social, and philosophical lenses, but a timeless warning. The disease, he reminds us, "never dies or disappears for good." It was an allegory for all recurring human crises.

Almost a century later, the world faced another invisible invader. COVID-19, like the plague of Oran, began as a medical catastrophe but soon revealed the vulnerabilities of many of the modern world's systems. The parallels between Camus's hypothetical epidemic and our own are striking. In both Oran and the modern world, ordinary routines collapsed almost overnight. Supply chains are disrupted, and grocery shelves are emptied, yet certain markets soar: home electronics, such as exercise bikes, streaming subscriptions, gaming platforms, and luxury goods, all reached new heights.

Just as Oran's routines fell apart, so too did those of modern life, albeit unevenly. The fractures ran along lines of class and vulnerability. In 2020, for example, the share price of Peloton, a maker of high-end exercise bikes, surged from $25 to a breathless $150, a sixfold increase in less than a year. While millions were losing their jobs, demand for high-end exercise bikes was exploding, a reminder that crises do not affect everyone the same. Likewise, alcohol consumption climbed, with many Americans increasingly choosing premium wines and spirits over cheaper alternatives.[3] Crisis revealed not only scarcity and anxiety but also the human impulse to seek pleasure and distraction, even when surrounded by uncertainty and loss. Fear, too, threatened both eras, and even the theological refrain that the plague was a form of God's punishment resurfaced almost unchanged.

Even though COVID-19 was a health crisis, it has had a long and lasting effect on global economies. The economic consequences of COVID-19 have been both widespread and profound, with world GDP contracting by 2.9%, a historic downturn matched only by the Great Depression and the 2008 financial crisis.

With the lockdowns taking effect in February and March of 2020, most businesses had to suspend operations for weeks, if not months. People were confined to their homes with nowhere to go. As a result, the travel industry, including airlines, railways, and agencies, began to lay off their employees. Companies such as airplane manufacturers like Boeing, airlines like Air Canada, travel companies like TripAdvisor, and airports such as Charlotte Douglas International Airport all laid off thousands. Theaters and film studios either decreased the number of employees or completely eliminated positions. Similarly, as schools are closed, many educational institutions like universities have restructured their staff and laid off large numbers.[4]

People were so afraid, or perhaps so overwhelmed, by the constant stream of alarming news, that they lost a clear sense of the scale of the crisis. Newspapers and television channels published daily counts of new infections and deaths. A consultancy firm, KEKST CNC, surveyed people from six countries: the United Kingdom, Sweden, Germany, France, the United States, and Japan, asking respondents a simple question: "How many people in your country have died from coronavirus?" The results were striking. Across all countries, respondents believed that up to 9% of the population had died from the virus, more than a hundred times higher than the official figures. In the United States, people thought that 30 million people had died, 225 times higher than reality; in Japan, the discrepancy was even more dramatic, with public estimates nearly a thousand times greater than the true numbers. This striking overestimation suggests how fear, uncertainty, and media coverage can distort public perception, turning a crisis into something that feels even more apocalyptic than it is.[5]

Before the COVID-19 pandemic, the world had never experienced a global economic crisis of this scale in over a century. In 2020, as the pandemic halted travel, disrupted supply chains, and closed shopping malls, nearly 90% of all countries experienced a simultaneous contraction in per capita gross domestic product (GDP) (Fig. 6.1). Only 23 countries out of 211 manage to avoid negative growth, a level of synchronized economic contraction that was unprecedented in modern history. The International Monetary Fund (IMF) announced in May 2020 that more than half of its member countries had applied for the emergency financing program, indicating the extent of financial strain countries were suffering from.[6]

The global impact of the pandemic was uneven. In 2020, sub-Saharan Africa saw GDP per capita contract by 4.5%, while the Euro area recorded an even steeper decline of 6.2%. Within Europe, certain countries suffered even more dramatic declines: Spain's 2020 GDP per capita plunged 11.4%,

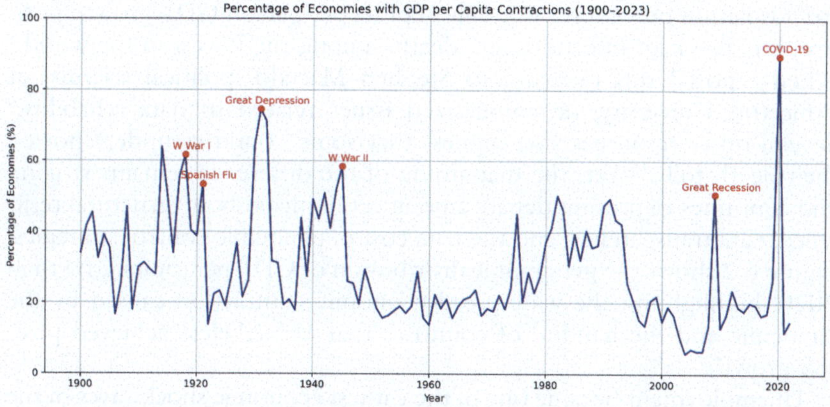

Fig. 6.1 Share of economies with GDP per capita contractions (1900–2023). The line graph illustrates the proportion of countries experiencing declines in GDP per capita each year. Major global downturns are depicted, including the disruptions of World War I, the Spanish flu (1918–1920), the Great Depression (1930s), World War II, the Great Recession (2008–2009), and the COVID-19 pandemic spike in 2020, where over 90% of economies contracted simultaneously. (Source: Prepared by Orhan Erdem, using data from Bolt and van Zanden [2025])

the United Kingdom's fell 10.5% (the steepest decline ever recorded by the UK's Office for National Statistics), and Greece's dropped 9%.[7] Across Africa, Libya endured the worst blow of all. Its GDP 2020 per capita collapsed by more than 30%, while the unemployment rate soared to 19%.

Yet, as stated above, 23 countries did manage to register positive per capita GDP growth in 2020. Bangladesh, China, Egypt, Vietnam, and Türkiye, for example, posted gains of 2.6, 2.1, 1.9, 1.9, and 0.88%, respectively. This stark divergence raises a compelling question: How did these countries, some of which are low-income, avoid contraction when nearly every high-income country (with Ireland being a notable exception) failed to grow?

We don't have a clear answer to this question. However, several factors may help explain this anomaly. First of all, countries like Vietnam and China implemented swift and aggressive lockdown measures. China's state-controlled economic mechanisms might have enabled an early recovery in the country's manufacturing and exports, and the government's capacity to mobilize resources efficiently accelerated the recovery. Vietnam's swift lockdowns, rigorous contact-tracing, targeted testing, and strict isolation procedures not only kept its per-person GDP growth positive, but also kept infections and deaths among the lowest in the world.[8] When I posed this question to Stephen Macedo, political scientist at Princeton University, he emphasized issues related to data reliability.[9] Several other resources also suggest that some countries underreported their death tolls.[10] Yet, the magnitude of the difference remains striking and continues to prompt debate among economists about structural resilience, data transparency, and the true cost of pandemic control strategies. Figure 6.2 shows the geographic distribution of GDP per capita growth in 2020, highlighting the widespread economic contraction caused by the pandemic and the handful of countries that nevertheless achieved positive growth.

Unemployment became one of the earliest economic shockwaves of the pandemic, sweeping through labor markets with astonishing speed. In the early months of 2020, as governments struggled to contain the spread of the virus, businesses went silent almost overnight. Lockdowns shuttered workplaces, grounded airplanes, and emptied office buildings. Thus, jobs that depended on physical presence did not gradually erode; they simply vanished. And it was the lowest-paid, least-protected workers who were the first to disappear from payrolls.

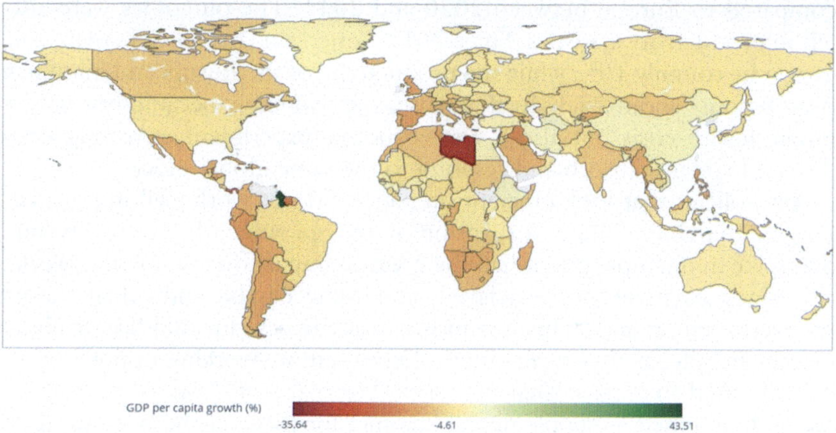

Fig. 6.2 2020 GDP per capita growth rates. This chart shows the annual GDP per capita growth rates in 2020, highlighting the widespread economic contraction during the COVID-19 pandemic. Countries that managed positive growth are shaded green; notable examples include China (2.1%), Türkiye (0.9%), Bangladesh (2.6%), and Vietnam (1.9%) in the East, and Ireland (5.8%) and Lithuania (0.07%) in the West. (Source: World Bank, World Development Indicators)

The numbers captured the scale of the collapse. In the United States, the unemployment rate soared to 14.8% in April, the highest level recorded since data collection began in 1948. It reached pre-pandemic levels only in 2022, two years after the introduction of lockdown measures. Europe experienced a similar trajectory, but the downturn was far less dramatic. Even though some countries experienced exceptionally high unemployment rates, reaching 18% in Greece and 16% in Spain, the Euro area as a whole peaked at a far more moderate 8.6%. The divergence between Europe and the United States reflected differences in economic philosophy. European governments acted quickly to preserve existing jobs, subsidizing wages to keep workers attached to their employers.[11] The United States took a different path: it allowed many jobs to disappear and instead delivered cash payments to households.

Those choices produced different labor market dynamics. According to *The Economist*, labor market reallocation, the rate at which workers shifted across jobs and industries, surged to twice the level in the United States compared to Europe between 2020 and 2022. The outcomes were also felt in productivity statistics. Since 2019, American labor productivity had grown by roughly 10%, while the productivity of the European Union has risen by only about 2%.[12] In this sense, the pandemic became not only a public health crisis but also a vast economic experiment, revealing how different systems absorb and respond to the same global shock.

Yet policies that look efficient on paper did not work well in practice. Despite the United States' expansion of unemployment benefits, this sudden spike in unemployment had the greatest impact on low-income workers. Many payments were delayed, and some eligible individuals never received them at all.[13] This was mostly not the case for middle- or high-income people, as they were either offered remote working opportunities or continued to receive their paycheck. For many of them, stimulus payments functioned as supplemental income; for those at the bottom, they were a fragile opportunity.

Globally, the trajectory shared a similar shape. Unemployment rates across the world soared in 2020, decreased slightly in 2021, and came to pre-pandemic levels only in 2022. But the global averages concealed important differences across national income groups.

The University of St. Gallen professor Charles Gottlieb and his co-authors approached this rupture from a truly global perspective, collecting data from 85 countries and asking a simple but revealing question: How does the same lockdown policy affect different economies? To answer it, they sorted the countries into five income groups, from the poorest to the richest quintile.[14]

Their findings showed a striking U-shaped pattern. According to their analysis, unemployment rates fell by 32% in the lowest income quintile of the distribution, 36% in the middle quintile, and 31% in the richest quintile. They concluded that lower-income countries experience a smaller decline compared to middle-income countries due to their dependence on essential activities, agriculture, basic manufacturing and logistics, which could not simply be paused.

GDP losses told a different story. While employment losses were U-shaped, GDP losses were not. In fact, the three lowest income quintiles experienced nearly identical contractions of around 39%, while the richest economies saw output fall by a smaller 31%. Essential sectors in low-income countries, especially agriculture, employ many workers but generate comparatively little value added. Thus, even when employment was partially preserved, output still collapsed. Richer countries, by contrast, maintain more productive sectors, such as finance, information and communication, and public administration, which were both essential and more compatible with remote work.

Stimulus Money and Government Intervention

The 2007–09 financial crisis exemplified that even the world's most market-oriented economies are willing to intervene in the markets when the stakes are high enough. In response to the crisis, the Federal Reserve Bank significantly expanded its assets by $3.7 trillion in the period from July 2007 to January 2015, effectively printing and injecting this amount into the financial system. The European Central Bank followed a similar path, injecting almost $3 trillion into the economy between August 2008 and May 2018.[15] Those were extraordinary actions at the time. Yet, what happened during the COVID-19 pandemic would eclipse them.

While labor markets were absorbing the shocks, another story was unfolding in the financial system. As unemployment surged and uncertainty spread, the Federal Reserve moved quickly to prevent the economy from collapsing. It slashed the interest rates to near zero and began purchasing government bonds at a pace far exceeding anything during the Great Recession. Fed officials repeatedly reassured the public that these extraordinary measures would stay in place until recovery was secure. For a while, inflation looked manageable, and officials dismissed rising prices as "transitory."

Behind the scenes, however, the scale of intervention was historic, larger than the response to the 2007–2009 financial crisis. Between January 2020 and April 2022, the Federal Reserve expanded its balance sheet by almost $4.8 trillion.[16] Although the phrase "printing money" is often used to describe this expansion, it is totally metaphorical, since the Fed doesn't print physical currency. Instead, the Fed created digital dollars to purchase assets such as Treasury bonds and mortgage-backed securities. These purchases made it easier and cheaper for the federal government to borrow, forming the financial backbone of its pandemic response.

This mechanism worked indirectly but effectively. Congress passed a series of enormous stimulus packages, such as direct payments to individuals, expanded unemployment benefits, and business support programs. To finance this spending, the Treasury issued new bonds. The Federal Reserve then bought large portions of those bonds, injecting newly created dollars into the financial system and helping the government sustain its relief efforts.

Yet, the benefits of these extraordinary measures flowed unevenly. Many asset owners used stimulus checks to invest in the stock market, thereby contributing to surging stock prices. By contrast, wage earners and low-income households largely used their stimulus checks to cover rent, food, and basic expenses, simply to stay afloat. The same policies that stabilized markets also widened existing inequalities.

In total, the U.S. Congress passed a series of six bills in response to the COVID-19 pandemic, all signed into law by President Donald Trump and, later, President Joe Biden.[17] The first and largest package was the CARES Act, which was signed into law on March 27, 2020.[18] This $2.1 trillion bill provided payments to individuals ($1200 per adult and $500 per child or $2400 for married couples), along with other unemployment benefits and support for businesses. Later that year, in December 2020, Congress passed a second major relief package (CRRSA Act), totaling $900 billion, which included $600 stimulus checks and unemployment assistance. The third major package, called the American Rescue Plan (ARP Act) and signed into law on March 11, 2021, which allocated $1.9 trillion in additional relief, including $1400 stimulus checks, and aid to state and local governments.

Combined with a few smaller relief measures, the total federal COVID-19 stimulus spending reached approximately $4.8 trillion by the end of the pandemic.,[1920] Of this, around $1.8 trillion went directly to individuals and families, $1.7 trillion to businesses, and $750 billion in aid to states and local governments, to support their efforts, such as education and transit, $480 billion was directed toward healthcare.[21] Not all of it reached its intended destination, though. Estimates suggest that 10% of pandemic-related stimulus money was lost to fraud, waste, and misuse, a reminder that in times of crises, speed often comes at the expense of precision.[22] In a recent case, U.S. federal prosecutors uncovered what they described as one of the largest pandemic-aid frauds: 59 people were convicted of siphoning nearly $1 billion of taxpayers' money into luxury purchases, real estate, and overseas transfers. This money was aimed at feeding children in need.[23]

The federal government financed this stimulus spending through borrowing, thus widening the budget deficit. While the official pre-pandemic projections put the 2020 at 4.6% of GDP, the actual figure soared to 14.7% of GDP once pandemic borrowing was included.,[2425] For comparison, during the 50 years prior to the pandemic, the average federal deficit was just 1.5% of GDP.

The United States was not alone in deploying extraordinary measures. Over the same period, in which the Federal Reserve increased its balance sheet by $4.8 trillion, the Eurosystem (the network of euro-area central banks led by the European Central Bank[26]) expanded its balance sheet by roughly $4 trillion. As French economist and Paris School of Economics professor Thomas Piketty has argued, large-scale money creation and the purchase of financial assets pushed up stock and property prices, which disproportionately enriched those at the top of the wealth distribution.[27]

In the United States, for example, house prices surged 26% in real terms between the end of 2019 and the end of 2023 (see Fig. 6.5). Globally, real house prices increased by about 11% over the same period. Equity markets told a similar story: adjusted for inflation, the S&P 500 index gained approximately 23%. The result was predictable. Asset holders emerged wealthier, reinforcing the dynamic that these kinds of extraordinary interventions, while stabilizing the economy, also amplify the existing inequalities.

Americans primarily used the first round of stimulus checks to cover expenses. As the crisis continued, however, the spending pattern changed. By the time second and third rounds were distributed, most households, nearly 80%, chose to save the money or pay down debt instead of spending it.[28] This shift is visible in Fig. 6.3: each spike corresponds to a major stimulus payment. The first sharp jump marks the initial round of checks at the end of March 2020; a second, slightly smaller peak follows the December 2020 payments, and the towering surge in early 2021 reflects the American Rescue Plan, the most generous of the three. Each stimulus wave temporarily lifted the disposable income far above its pre-pandemic trend (shown by the dashed line). Once the payment stopped, however, incomes fell back down, and for much of 2021 and 2022, they dipped below the projected trend.

The stimulus money genuinely helped households in the short term. For example, the overall poverty rate in the U.S. decreased from 2020 to 2021, with an even more dramatic reduction in child poverty. Yet the figure also explains why these gains did not last. Because the increases in disposable income were driven by one-time transfers rather than permanent changes in earnings, their effects faded quickly as the payments ended. By 2023 and 2024, poverty levels bounced back to levels even higher than before the pandemic.[29] The temporary spikes in income,

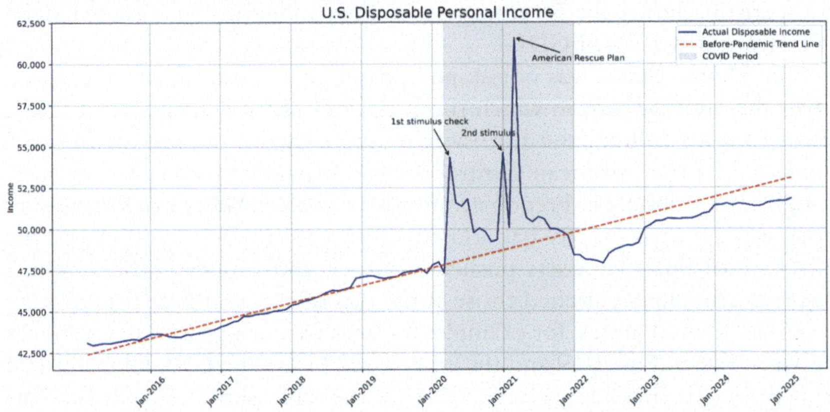

Fig. 6.3 U.S. disposable personal income. This chart displays monthly U.S. disposable income (in terms of 2017 dollars). The solid blue line represents actual income levels, while the dashed line shows a projected trend based on pre-pandemic data (February 2015–February 2020). Shaded in gray is the COVID-19 period (March 2020–January 2022). Key stimulus payments are annotated. Despite this temporary support, disposable income levels never returned to the pre-pandemic trend. (Source: U.S. Bureau of Economic Analysis, Real Disposable Personal Income: Per Capita [A229RX0], retrieved from FRED, Federal Reserve Bank of St. Louis; https://fred.stlouisfed.org/series/A229RX0)

dramatic as they were, could not counterbalance the structural problems that emerged because of the pandemic.

Leaving the side effects of government intervention to the following chapter, I want to focus on the economic fault line that the pandemic deepened: debt and inflation.

The excessive stimulus packages during COVID-19 had two direct effects on the economy of the countries that implemented them: First, they increased the debt levels in many countries. Public debt, often referred to as government debt, represents the total amount a government owes to domestic and foreign creditors. It accumulates when governments borrow to finance budget deficits, fund infrastructure projects, or respond to crises such as economic recessions. A rising debt-to-GDP ratio indicates that a country's debt is growing faster than its economic output. According to the IMF, one-third of countries, representing 80% of global GDP, now have public debt levels that are not only higher than they were before the pandemic but are also increasing more rapidly.[30] The global average public debt-to-GDP ratio reached 98.7% in 2020, the highest level recorded since 1900, and climbed to 110% for advanced economies. Although the global average declined slightly to 94.7% by 2025, it is projected to surpass 100% by 2030.[31]

In 2020 alone, several countries defaulted on their sovereign debt, including Ecuador ($800 million), Argentina ($63 billion), Belize, Suriname, Lebanon, and Zambia.,[3233] Defaulting on loans typically leads to a decline in a country's sovereign rating, forcing it to borrow even at a higher interest rate in the future. This further increases the debt burden of countries, leading to a vicious cycle of rising debt and declining creditworthiness. A March 2020 lockdown in Gambia led to 50% crop losses, while food inflation rose to double digits. The Gambian government borrowed about $10 million in emergency funds, plus $21.3 million in IMF loans, while tax revenue halved.

These debts will ultimately be borne by future generations. The young people who were deprived of a proper education during the COVID-19 pandemic now face the additional burden of repaying the massive public debts accumulated during the same period. In effect, the pandemic imposed a double burden on the shoulders of the current young generation: it left students with significant learning loss (see Chapter 8: Educationally Yours) in the present, while simultaneously handing them the bill for the enormous public debts accumulated in response to the emergency. Of course, this debt problem did not originate with the pandemic alone. Earlier shocks, most notably the 2007–2009 financial crisis, had added to the debts of the nations. But the pandemic undeniably intensified the challenge, leaving a heavier bill for those who had the least control over the events that created it.

The second major scar of the pandemic was inflation. At the very beginning, prices actually fell as consumer demand dropped drastically. A dramatic example came in April 2020, when oil prices actually turned negative, an almost unthinkable event. When travel came to a halt and factories shut down, the demand for oil disappeared overnight. Yet production had not slowed quickly enough, creating a massive surplus. Oil had to be stored somewhere, and, by April, most available storage, especially in places like Cushing, Oklahoma, was full. Traders who had contracts to receive oil in May had nowhere to put it. Desperate to avoid taking physical delivery, they sold those contracts at a loss, pushing prices below zero.

But this calm did not last long. As described above, governments injected record-breaking amounts of money into their economies. In the United States, personal incomes soared during the pandemic not because of wage growth but because of stimulus checks, expanded unemployment benefits, and business support packages. At first, much of this money was saved for precautionary reasons. With demand still muted, inflation appeared controlled, prompting Federal Reserve officials to describe the early price increases as "transitory."

Over time, however, those savings were converted into spending, which eventually fueled inflation. When that wave of spending met supply chain disruption, labor shortages, and constrained production capacity, inflation began to accelerate. Global manufacturing stopped when a severe semiconductor shortage spread through industries as diverse as automobiles and consumer electronics. Automobile companies such as Nissan and Mercedes struggled to find chips for their cars.[34] At the same time, the historic shipping-container shortage and repeated bottlenecks at major ports sent freight costs soaring and delayed goods for weeks. According to a survey by Ernst & Young, 57% of U.S. companies reported being severely affected because their supply chains lacked resilience; in addition, nearly half experienced major workforce disruptions.[35]

In the United States, millions of workers left their jobs in what became known as the "Great Resignation," creating severe labor shortages in many sectors.[36] For example, school districts across the country began offering large signing bonuses to recruit bus drivers and other critical staff.[37] With too few workers available, businesses were forced to raise wages to attract and retain employees, adding to inflation in ways few had anticipated.

By November 2021, however, inflation began rising, and the labor market was booming. Fed officials changed their view that inflation was transitory, concluding that it was a persistent phenomenon. Thus, they abruptly ended asset purchases by March 2022 and launched one of the fastest rate-hike cycles in modern history.

Several studies highlight how this mix of labor shortages, borrowing, and supply disruptions fueled the post-pandemic surge in prices. An IMF report shows that in the U.S., tight labor markets alone added about 2 percentage points to core inflation, while rising energy costs and supply chain problems contributed another 4.6 percentage points.[38] Another IMF study finds that local labor shortages were behind nearly 70% of the jump in services inflation in late 2022 and early 2023, showing just how hard it is to bring prices back down when the job market remains so tight.[39]

This inflationary surge primarily affected countries that implemented massive stimulus packages, such as the U.S. and some European countries. Asian countries, however, followed a very different path (See Fig. 6.4). Their governments generally provided smaller direct cash transfers and relied more on targeted government subsidies.[40] As a result, consumer demand did not spike as much as it did in the U.S., and supply chains recovered more quickly in many Asian economies.

By the end of 2022, the Federal Reserve had raised interest rates from near zero to 5–5.25 percent through ten consecutive hikes. In mid-2022, it also started shrinking its $9 trillion balance sheet.[41] The strategy largely worked: inflation eased by the beginning of 2023, without a spike in unemployment. However, they couldn't avoid the criticisms for being too late.

The pandemic reshaped real estate markets in unexpected ways. In most crises, real estate cools and slows as people tighten their belts and uncertainty settles over the economy. Yet, COVID-19 produced the opposite outcome. Instead of contracting, inflation-adjusted house prices surged across much of the world (Fig. 6.5).[42] Some countries saw

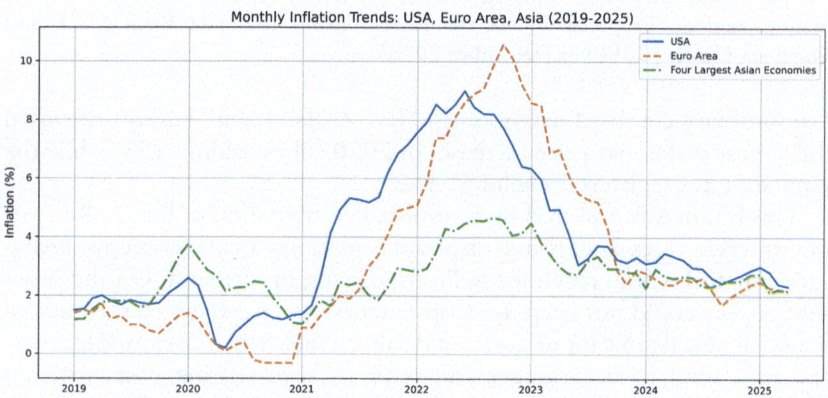

Fig. 6.4 Inflation trends in the U.S., Euro Area, and the four largest Asian economies, 2019–2025. The four largest Asian economies consist of China, India, Japan, and South Korea. (Source: Prepared by Orhan Erdem using data from Federal Reserve Bank of St. Louis (FRED), IMF, and Eurostat)

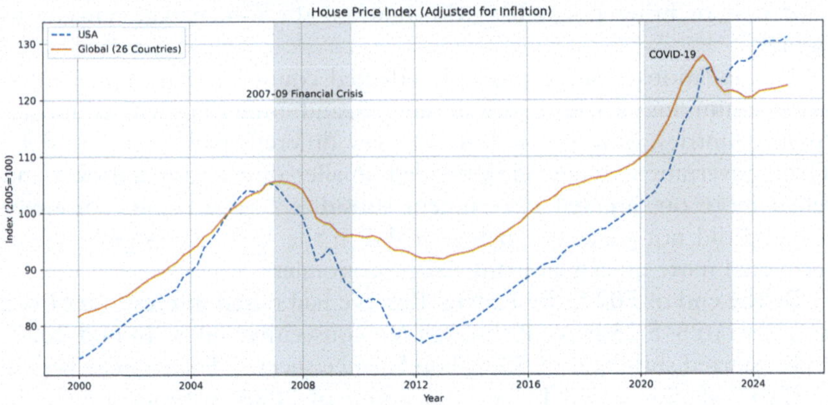

Fig. 6.5 Global vs U.S. real house price indices (adjusted for inflation). This chart compares real house price indices for the U.S. (blue, dashed) and an average across 26 countries (solid, orange) from the 2020s to 2025. The shaded areas highlight two major disruptions: the 2007–2009 financial crisis and the onset of the COVID-19 pandemic in 2020. Following COVID-19, both indices exhibit sharp upward trends, reflecting rapid house price appreciation, which is more pronounced in the U.S., driven by factors such as record-low interest rates, increased savings, and demand shifts due to remote work. This divergence illustrates how the pandemic intensified housing market pressures, particularly in the United States. (Source: Prepared by Orhan Erdem using the data from Mack and Martínez-García [2011] in December 2025)

extraordinary climbs: Luxembourg, New Zealand, and Türkiye recorded the largest real house price increases in 2020, all exceeding 15%, while the United States registered a solid 5% rise.

This boom was powered by an unusual combination of forces. Record-low interest rates and rising disposable incomes made homeownership suddenly feel within reach for millions, driving up demand. On the other side, supply could not keep up. Construction was slowed by a shortage of materials, escalating input costs, and labor constraints. Meanwhile, renters, who tend to be younger and poorer, faced soaring costs with no equivalent wealth gain. The real estate developers could not find enough workers for the construction. Projects that once took months stretched into years. Together, these factors created perfect conditions for a rapid rise in house prices.[43]

However, the pace of price growth was not uniform across U.S. cities and states. States with either very high or very low stringency measures, such as lockdowns and mask mandates, experienced smaller price increases compared to states with moderate levels of stringency. One study I am involved with indicates that these extremely stringent states saw a net negative immigration rate, as many people preferred to relocate to states with moderate measures.[44] In the case of the cities, people preferred to relocate from city centers to suburban areas as they sought larger, cheaper suburban housing, increasing the house prices in the suburbs.[45] Thus, suburban areas saw significant population increases, whereas urban areas experienced population declines. In the U.S., median house prices had already been increasing faster than the median income before the pandemic, but this gap widened significantly after COVID-19.[46]

Lost Decade of Poverty Reduction

Leonard Cohen's song "Everybody Knows" echoes an old truth: "Everybody knows the fight was fixed. The poor stay poor, the rich get rich." Crises widen divides long before they heal them. The pandemic didn't just bring a virus; it stressed the invisible bonds that keep daily life functioning. Supply chains cracked, local markets were shut down, and lockdowns swept across continents, creating a shock that weighed most heavily on the shoulders of the disadvantaged and poor. As the world economies rebalanced, evidence of this disruption began to emerge. Not only across countries, but also in the lives of ordinary individuals.

By October 2020, once the initial panic was over, the University of Oxford's Department of Social Policy and Intervention warned that "poverty and inequality will potentially increase right across Europe, with poor workers losing as much as 16% of income and social cohesion between countries also being damaged by pandemic lockdown measures."[47] Evidence of this shift was already visible. In Madrid, a food bank that typically served about 400 people a month before the pandemic announced that they suddenly started to distribute ten tons of supplies daily to some 3500 people. Organizers called it a "new wave of poverty," a phrase that captured the widening cracks in society.[48]

If this were the reality in one of the world's wealthiest regions, imagine what happened elsewhere. The picture was far darker across low- and middle-income countries. According to the United Nations, 10,000 children died every month in 2020 from hunger linked to the economic and social disruptions caused by restrictions. Market closures and supply chain breakdowns cut off millions of families from food supplies. In Burkina Faso, Venezuela, Afghanistan, Yemen, and Sudan, infants were pushed to the very edge of famine. Prices soared, reaching 136% inflation in Sudan, while in Venezuela, some children died after surviving for weeks on near-starvation diets.[49]

In Senegal, lockdowns devastated much of the economy. After lockdowns were imposed in March 2020, thousands risked their lives to leave the country for the Canary Islands, nearly 1000 miles away from Senegal's coast, in search of livelihood and opportunity. Many died on the way.[50] Spanish authorities report that in 2020, the number of migrants arriving in the Canary Islands rose nearly tenfold, from 2687 in 2019 to about 23,000.[51] West African historian Toby Green reports, in his book *The Covid Consensus*, that the proportion of South Africans who experienced hunger at some point in 2020 more than doubled from the previous year, reaching 47%.

In India, *The Telegraph* described a similar picture: the lockdown triggered a devastating hunger crisis, pushing an estimated 400 million people deeper into poverty. Malnutrition rates soared, and doctors reported widespread undernourishment. The death of five-year-old Sonia Kumari, who starved to death, symbolized how the pandemic's economic fallout proved as deadly as the virus itself. These tragedies revealed a painful truth: the poorer the country, the less room it had to cushion the crisis.

Poverty is often defined as the proportion of the population living below a certain level of income. Because this level can vary by institution and country, poverty can be measured in a variety of ways, reflecting different economic circumstances. One method the World Bank uses defines poverty as living on less than $3 a day.[52] This level aims to capture the minimal income required for adequate food, shelter, and essentials. This $3 is expressed in 2021 purchasing power parity (PPP), which ensures that this threshold reflects the same real standard of living as $3 would buy in the United States in 2021. Because prices differ from country to country, the equivalent local currency amount needed to match this purchasing power varies. For example, three dollars in Finland cannot buy the same amount of goods as three dollars in Türkiye, where prices are generally lower. As a result, the equivalent amount in each country's currency varies, but it always represents a comparable level of purchasing power. The World Bank, which was established in 1944, has been working to reduce poverty since then. That's their self-defined sole job.

As a result of all the economic fallout in 2020, the poverty rate defined above, which had steadily declined from 38% in 1998 to 11% in 2018, increased for the first time in decades in 2020. The fight against global poverty has slowed because of the pandemic. The World Bank warns that at the current rate, its target level of a 3% poverty rate has become out of reach.[53]

According to the African Development Bank, the pandemic pushed about 30 million Africans into poverty in 2020 alone. Around the world, about 838 million people now live in extreme poverty.[54] Although the poverty rate started going down after the pandemic, it has not recovered the momentum it had before. Many reports now refer to 2020–30 as "a lost decade" for poverty reduction.[55] Behind these statistics were millions of lives affected, often permanently.

Economic Inequality

> We may have democracy, or we may have wealth concentrated in the hands of a few, but we can't have both.
> —Louis D. Brandeis, U.S. Supreme Court Justice, 1941

If poverty tells us who fell into crisis first, inequality tells us who has tall ladders and who has short ones to climb back, and who has none at all. Crises are an inevitable part of modern economic and social life. In just the twenty-first century alone, we have faced the 2007/2008 financial crisis, the COVID-19 pandemic in 2020, and the Russia–Ukraine war in 2022. One pattern repeats itself across all these shocks: the gap between high and low earners widens. This is a well-documented trend in research and is easy to understand in real life.[56] Low-income earners are the first to lose their jobs, they have the fewest savings to lean on, and they receive the least support when systems come under stress. When a crisis hits, those already living close to the edge are first to fall, while those with stable jobs, stable incomes, assets, and financial cushions often get through the crisis with far less damage.

Werner Troesken's *The Pox of Liberty* shows that infectious disease outcomes are not determined by money alone. The same rules that promote liberty and economic growth can also slow decisive public health action, creating vulnerabilities that fall disproportionately on the poor. His historical analysis of yellow fever and smallpox offers a powerful framework for understanding COVID-19: the pandemic exposed the strengths and weaknesses of democratic governance and longstanding inequalities.[57] COVID-19 illuminated weaknesses with brutal clarity.

These vulnerabilities did not emerge with COVID-19; they were old cracks in the system. Even tax policies, introduced over decades, quietly shifted the burden downward. In the U.S., for example, the total tax rates as a percentage of income for the lowest income group rose from 16% in 1950 to 27% in 2018, whereas the same rate for the top 400 earners in the country declined from 70% to 23% over the same period.[58] In other words, even in the absence of crises, the tax burden on the poorest has increased, while that on the richest has fallen, further exacerbating economic inequality. This widening gap creates a landscape where the poor enter crises already weakened, with less savings, less political voice, and almost no cushions against shocks.

While the economic inequality gap was already a problem across the world before the pandemic, it has been exacerbated in the aftermath. It imposed its heaviest toll on the world's poorest. Tourism collapsed, and even a recovery in 2022–2023 only reached 30% of pre-pandemic levels. Tourism employs millions of low-wage workers across developing countries. When that sector collapsed, these incomes disappeared too.

Income inequality refers to the unequal distribution of annual earnings among individuals in a particular country, over a specific period, typically a year. Income can come from labor (such as wages, salaries, and bonuses) and from capital (such as interest, rents, and profits). High levels of income inequality suggest a wide gap between earners, i.e., while a small group of people earn significantly high incomes, a significant portion of people struggle to meet basic living expenses.

In contrast, wealth inequality refers to the unequal distribution of accumulated financial and nonfinancial assets, such as homes, stocks, retirement accounts, business ownership, and savings minus debt. Wealth is more enduring than income and typically exceeds income because it reflects not just what people earn in a year, but also what they have accumulated over time through savings and capital gains. Importantly, wealth can generate passive income and compound over generations, such as home rents.

To grasp the scale of the difference between income and wealth, consider the following: In 2021, global income amounted to $122 trillion, while global net wealth reached a staggering $724 trillion, nearly six times higher.[59] This enormous gap highlights how wealth accumulates far beyond annual earnings.

Now, let's take a closer look at how this income and wealth are distributed globally, and how the COVID-19 pandemic disrupted these patterns.

Wealth Inequality

Over the thirty years from 1994 to 2024, the total household net worth in the United States increased more than sixfold, reaching $161 trillion. Yet this astonishing wealth has not been equally shared across society. The benefits have flowed disproportionately to those already at the top of the wealth ladder. In particular, the top 0.1% of Americans, roughly 130,000 households, have steadily expanded their share of national wealth. COVID-19 did not change this trajectory; it accelerated it.

The COVID-19 pandemic further exacerbated this inequality, driving the wealth share for the richest Americans to the highest level in history. By 2024, the top 0.1% of Americans controlled 14% of the country's total wealth. In stark contrast, the bottom 50% of the population collectively owned just 2.5% of the national wealth (Fig. 6.6). While the bottom 50% of the population did see a modest increase in their share of wealth compared to pre-pandemic levels, thanks in part to stimulus payments and temporary government support, their gains were marginal when compared with those experienced by the top 0.1%.

Globally, the picture was much the same. The wealthiest individuals and families around the world saw their wealth grow during the pandemic, often fueled by increasing stock prices and rising real estate values. According to a report by UBS, the Swiss multinational investment bank, billionaire wealth surged by 27.5% in just four months, between April and July 2020, reaching a record $10.2 trillion at the height of the crisis.[60]

Meanwhile, the economic fallout of the pandemic, lost jobs, disrupted schooling, and insufficient healthcare access, hit low-income populations and developing nations the hardest. By 2021, the most recent year for which global data is available, the top 0.1% of the world population, roughly 5 million people, controlled 11% of total global wealth. Figure 6.6 highlights how this extreme concentration of wealth in the hands of a tiny elite has been evolving before and after the pandemic. The global economic system continued to reward capital ownership far more than labor, despite the government support.

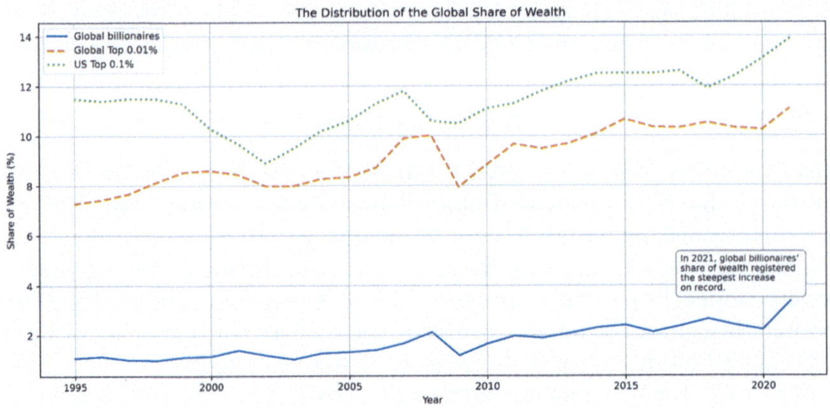

Fig. 6.6 The distribution of the global share of wealth. The global top 0.01%, approximately 520,000 people in 2021, increased their share of total wealth from 7% in 1995 to 11% in 2021. Meanwhile, global billionaires, defined as individuals with net assets exceeding $1 billion, also saw a surge in their collective share, with 2021 marking the steepest annual increase on record. In the U.S., the top 0.1% saw their wealth share climb to 13.9% in 2021. The most recent estimate, from 2024 (not shown in the chart), is 14.0%. Wealth is measured as the net sum of financial (e.g., stocks, bonds) and non-financial (e.g., real estate) assets, minus debts. (Sources: U.S. data: Federal Reserve Bank of St. Louis and Financial Accounts of the U.S. (Z-1). Global data: [Chancel et al., 2022])

Income Inequality

Globally, the bottom 40% of earners saw their incomes fall by an average of 4%, twice as severe as the losses experienced by the wealthiest 20%.[61] Consequently, global inequality widened for the first time in decades. The pandemic did not create inequality, but it accelerated it, even after the stimulus payments.

A 2021 study published in Science Advances by 26 researchers reviewed 30,000 households from nine low- and middle-income countries[62] in Africa, Asia, and Latin America to understand the economic consequences of the pandemic.[63] The authors found a median income decline of nearly 70%. The consequences were immediate and visceral: hunger surged across entire regions. In Sierra Leone, 87% of rural households reported skipping meals; in Bangladesh, 69% of landless laborers did the same. Even in relatively better-off Colombia, 87% of respondents reported income losses, and over half faced food insecurity. Children were hit the hardest; rates of missed or reduced meals rose by roughly two-thirds. Local enterprises in Kenya and Sierra Leone saw profits collapse by half. Only one in ten households received any government or NGO assistance. The researchers warned that such shocks would not vanish with the virus.

In the U.S., the income gap across races also widened. Even though the average income level generally rose between 2019 and 2022, this mainly benefited white families. According to a 2023 Federal Reserve paper, white families in the U.S. saw a modest 1% increase between 2019 and 2022. In contrast, the typical Black family's income declined by 2%,[64] and Hispanic families experienced a 1% drop.

This is mainly explained by the overrepresentation of Black and Hispanic individuals in "essential jobs," such as food delivery, nursing, and other frontline services, that exposed them to higher health and economic risks while offering less protection. In other words, while economically advantaged people could afford to stay home, others had to work and provide food for all. COVID-19 didn't create economic fault lines; it simply widened them.

Businesses

The business world followed the same pattern. Small and non-white businesses were hit the hardest, with small businesses far more likely than large firms to shut down permanently. Black-owned firms experienced closure rates more than twice those of white-owned counterparts.[65] Between February and April 2020, closures were steep among Black-owned firms (41%), compared with Hispanic-owned (32%), Asian-owned (26%), and white-owned businesses (17%). Black businesses were disproportionately located in COVID hot spots and had weaker access to relief: in many counties with dense Black-owned activity, fewer than 20% of firms received Paycheck Protection Program loans.[66] In other words, the pandemic rewarded scale and punished vulnerability.

Financial Markets

On August 12, 2020, the UK's Office for National Statistics of the UK released the figures for the country's second quarter growth. The economy contracted by 21.9%. The wording of the newspapers was as dramatic as the contraction rate: "UK GDP collapsed," "UK GDP plunged," "UK

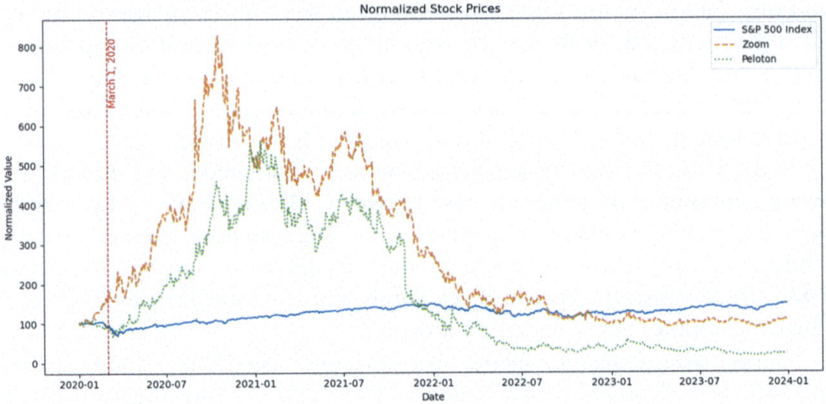

Fig. 6.7 Normalized performance of S&P 500, Zoom and Peloton (2020–2024). This chart displays the normalized index level of the S&P 500 (solid blue line), alongside the normalized stock prices of Zoom (dashed orange) and Peloton (dotted green) from early 2020 through the end of 2023. A vertical red dashed line marks March 1, 2020, showing the early onset of COVID-19's market impact. While both companies saw significant gains due to increased remote activity and home fitness demand, their market values declined and even, in Peloton's case, fell well below pre-pandemic levels after 2022

records largest-ever quarterly fall." They were right. It was the largest slump in the UK's history of statistics. It couldn't have been worse. However, a more stunning thing came later that day. When the stock market closed that day, the FTSE 100, the benchmark index of the 100 largest companies listed on the London Stock Exchange, had risen by 2.04%. It was a surreal moment: the real economy was collapsing, yet financial markets were marching upward.

Across the Atlantic, the United States witnessed a different but familiar pattern. The S&P 500 index dropped by 33% between mid-February and mid-March. It took until mid-August for the market index to climb back to where it stood before the drop. However, COVID-19 reshaped stock markets wildly. Companies well-suited to the needs of the pandemic era, such as Zoom, a videoconferencing platform, and Peloton, a producer of at-home fitness equipment, soared in value. The share price of Zoom saw a more than sevenfold increase in the first nine months of 2020. However, these inflated valuations proved temporary; by 2025, their market values had either returned to their pre-pandemic values, if not fallen lower (Fig. 6.7).

Who Paid the Price?

Historical experience over the past century suggests that major financial crises leave long-lasting effects: on average, it takes about eight years for income levels to return to their pre-crisis levels.[67] While advanced economies tend to recover more quickly, developing nations suffer. The World Bank expects high-income countries to return to their pre-pandemic per capita levels by 2027.

The situation is significantly different for developing economies. In many of these countries, pandemic-related disruptions have compounded pre-existing structural weaknesses. As a result, the per capita income growth of emerging market and developing economies (EMDE) between 2025 and 2027 is still expected to be at least 5 percentage points less than their pre-pandemic levels. Excluding China, it might take these countries two decades to fully recover the economic setbacks of the 2020s.[68]

Center for Strategic & International Studies (CSIS) reports that in 2020, international financial institutions, such as the IMF and the World Bank Group, approved $240 billion in financial aid. However, only $12 billion of that reached low-income countries.[69] In other words, those most in need received the least support. This unequal and disproportional distribution of global relief raises serious concerns about deepening global inequality. While high-income countries had fiscal space and monetary tools to launch massive stimulus efforts, many low-income countries were left to struggle with the pandemic's aftereffects with far fewer resources.

Such disparities point to a troubling outcome: the pandemic is likely to have widened the already significant income gap between nations. The rich, with wider access to capital and support tools, stood to recover more quickly, if not emerge even stronger, while the poor faced steeper and prolonged hardships. The pandemic did not distribute the suffering evenly. In COVID-19's case, however, the poor, within and across nations, bore the deepest scars.

Notes

1. Camus and Gilbert (1991, p. 37)
2. Camus and Gilbert (1991, p. 308)
3. Sullivan (2020)
4. Voytko-Best (2020)

5. https://www.kekstcnc.com/media/2793/kekstcnc_research_covid-19_opinion_tracker_wave-4.pdf
6. https://www.imf.org/en/News/Articles/2020/05/21/tr052120-transcript-of-imf-press-briefing
7. Office for National Statistics (2021)
8. https://www.imf.org/en/News/Articles/2021/03/09/na031021-vietnam-successfully-navigating-the-pandemic
9. https://www.youtube.com/watch?v=OwfQy1-qya8 min 19:45.
10. https://www.economist.com/graphic-detail/2022/08/03/covid-19-has-damaged-the-reputation-of-cuban-health-care
11. Eymeoud et al. (2021)
12. https://www.economist.com/finance-and-economics/2025/11/10/recessions-have-become-ultra-rare-that-is-storing-up-trouble
13. https://www.cnbc.com/2020/04/20/amid-pandemic-unemployment-checks-can-take-longer-to-arrive.html
14. Gottlieb et al. (2022)
15. Erdem (2020a)
16. https://fred.stlouisfed.org/series/WALCL
17. https://pandemicoversight.gov/about-us/pandemic-relief-program-laws
18. https://www.congress.gov/bill/116th-congress/house-bill/748
19. Update: Three rounds of stimulus checks. See how many went out and for how much. | Pandemic Oversight
20. U.S. Government Accountability Office (2023)
21. https://www.nytimes.com/interactive/2022/03/11/us/how-covid-stimulus-money-was-spent.html
22. https://apnews.com/article/pandemic-fraud-waste-billions-small-business-labor-fb1d9a9eb24857efbe4611344311ae78
23. https://www.nytimes.com/2025/11/29/us/fraud-minnesota-somali.html
24. Congress of the United States Congressional Budget Office (2020)
25. Congress of the United States Congressional Budget Office (2020)
26. https://fred.stlouisfed.org/series/ECBASSETSW
27. Piketty and Couper (2021, p. 320)
28. https://www.pgpf.org/article/how-did-americans-spend-their-stimulus-checks-and-how-did-it-affect-the-economy/
29. The U.S. Census Bureau reports poverty using two measures: the official poverty rate and the supplemental poverty measure (SPM). Researchers tend to use SPM because it "uses after-tax income, includes refundable tax credits, includes the value of noncash benefits, and subtracts certain expenses from income." According to the Census Bureau, the SPM poverty rate decreased from 9.2% in 2020 to 7.8% in 2021, before rising sharply, to 12.9%, in 2024. Child poverty followed a similar pattern. It

decreased from 9.7% in 2020 to 5.2% in 2021 and surged to 13.4% in 2024. Notably, neither measure has returned to its 2019 level. https://www.census.gov/library/publications/2025/demo/p60-287.html

30. Dabla-Norris and Furceri (2025)
31. See Figures 7.1, 7.2, and 7.3 at https://rogoff.scholars.harvard.edu/time-different%E2%80%94data-files for data from 1900 to 2007 and https://www.imf.org/external/datamapper/GGXWDG_NGDP@WEO/WEOWORLD from 2007 on.
32. https://www.cnn.com/2020/08/04/investing/argentina-debt-deal/index.html
33. https://www.ft.com/content/35c58b5f-f890-4390-967a-28c0a0a1fb50
34. https://www.reuters.com/business/autos-transportation/nissan-mercedes-sound-alarm-over-chip-supply-crisis-2025-10-29/
35. https://www.ey.com/en_us/insights/supply-chain/how-covid-19-impacted-supply-chains-and-what-comes-next
36. Cohen (2021); Hsu (2021)
37. Kamenetz (2021)
38. Ball et al. (2022)
39. Chen et al. (2024)
40. https://www.brookings.edu/wp-content/uploads/2024/08/WP97_Fatas.pdf
41. https://www.federalreserve.gov/econres/notes/feds-notes/the-federal-reserves-responses-to-the-post-covid-period-of-high-inflation-20240214.html
42. For the income, see *The Pandemic Paradox* by Fulford, p. 43.
43. https://www.imf.org/en/-/media/files/publications/gfsr/2021/october/english/text.pdf
44. Erdem and Gider (2025)
45. Delventhal et al. (2022); D'Lima et al. (2022); Gupta et al. (2022)
46. In 2019, the median house cost was 4.6 times the median income; by 2021, this ratio had increased to 5.4.
47. https://www.ox.ac.uk/news/2020-10-29-poverty-and-inequality-surge-across-europe-wake-covid-19
48. https://www.reuters.com/article/world/madrid-food-bank-swamped-by-new-wave-of-poverty-idUSKBN27F2LH/
49. https://apnews.com/article/virus-outbreak-africa-ap-top-news-understanding-the-outbreak-hunger-5cbee9693c52728a3808f4e7b4965cbd
50. Green (2021, pp. 131–132)
51. https://www.infomigrants.net/en/post/29909/spain-new-migrant-camps-in-the-canary-islands

52. In 2025, World Bank's Poverty and Inequality Platform has revised the global poverty rate from $2.15 per day to $3.00.
53. Global poverty and climate goals will remain out of reach with business-as-usual policies
54. Lønborg et al. (2025)
55. https://blogs.worldbank.org/en/opendata/the-polycrisis-behind-a-lost-decade-of-poverty-reduction
56. Woo (2023); Zewde and Crystal (2022)
57. Troesken (2015)
58. https://taxjusticenow.org/
59. Chancel et al. (2022)
60. https://www.ubs.com/content/dam/static/noindex/wealth-management/ubs-billionaires-report-2020-spread.pdf
61. https://www.worldbank.org/en/news/press-release/2022/10/05/global-progress-in-reducing-extreme-poverty-grinds-to-a-halt
62. The nine developing countries included in the study are Burkina Faso, Ghana, Kenya, Rwanda, and Sierra Leone in Africa; Bangladesh, Nepal, and the Philippines in Asia; and Colombia in Latin America.
63. Egger et al. (2021)
64. Aladangady et al. (2023)
65. Fairlie et al. (2023)
66. Mills and Battisto (2020)
67. Reinhart and Rogoff (2014)
68. *Global Economic Prospects, June 2025* (2025)
69. https://www.csis.org/analysis/international-financial-institutions-covid-19-approvals-approach-240-billion-2020

CHAPTER 7

Politically Yours

Abstract This chapter examines the political transformations triggered by the pandemic, focusing on shifts in governance, public trust, and institutional power. It explores how emergency measures expanded state authority, sometimes leading to increased authoritarian tendencies. At the same time, it analyzes how government responses influenced public confidence, polarization, and political stability, suggesting that COVID-19 has left a lasting imprint on democratic and political systems worldwide.

Keywords Politics • Governance • State power • Polarization • Public policy • Civil liberties • Authoritarianism

If COVID-19 had been an experiment, it would have revealed many political consequences. For example, it would have shown how easily governments could expand their authoritarian reach, curb individual freedoms, and restrict society from hard-won rights, such as liberty, education, despite centuries of progress. As Albert Camus warned in *The Plague*—"They fancied themselves free, and no one will ever be free so long as there are pestilences,"[1] a reminder that freedom often proves fragile in the face of disease. Obviously, it was no experiment, but we all witnessed these things unfold.

Almost 10 years before the pandemic, in 2008, the ACLU (the American Civil Liberties Union) published a report entitled *Pandemic Preparedness: The Need for a Public Health—Not A Law Enforcement/*

O. Erdem, *The Socioeconomic Impact of Pandemics*,
https://doi.org/10.1007/978-3-032-24189-4_7

National Security—Approach. There was no COVID, no serious global threat, but their warning could have been written during the COVID-19 pandemic. It reads: "The lessons from history should be kept in mind whenever we are told by government officials that 'tough', liberty-limiting actions are needed to protect us from dangerous diseases."[2]

The political arena before COVID-19 was already fragile, marked by a surge in nationalistic sentiment worldwide. The pandemic arrived at a moment almost tailor-made for the COVID rhetoric of losing borders. Thus, most governments did not miss the opportunity to do so and framed the crisis around caring for the nation first.

Many governments used COVID-19 as an excuse to expand their authoritative reach. For example, China relied on digital tracking systems to monitor citizens' movements. Chinese authorities have been utilizing an extensive surveillance infrastructure, with 700 million cameras across the country, mostly equipped with facial recognition technology.[3] They spend more than $6.6 million every year on monitoring and shaping online content.[4] These systems continuously monitor and record the location and behavior of their 1.4 billion citizens. In other words, China has one camera for every two people. Their social credit system leverages this surveillance data to assess individual behavior. Depending on their credit score, citizens might receive benefits or penalties, such as easier access to loans or travel restrictions.

In Hungary, the country's parliament granted Prime Minister Viktor Orbán sweeping emergency powers to respond to the crisis in April 2020. Under the justification of combating the pandemic, the Hungarian parliament authorized the government to suspend existing laws, implement rule by decree, and postpone elections indefinitely. In addition, the law permitted the jailing of persons deemed to be spreading "falsehoods" or "distorted truths" that interfere with the pandemic response, up to five years' imprisonment.[5] What begins as a health measure turned out to be an instrument of unchecked power. By 2018, even before COVID-19, the Swedish-based V-Dem Institute had already classified Hungary as an electoral authoritarian regime, a label the pandemic measures only reinforced.

In Slovenia, thousands of protestors gathered in Ljubljana, accusing the government of using the pandemic as an excuse to restrict freedoms. They denounced its policies as those of a "modern occupier," warning of a growing degradation of democracy.[6]

In the Philippines, President Rodrigo Duterte declared a nationwide "state of calamity" in March 2020; he later extended it for another year, citing the need to access emergency funds quickly and the use of police and military forces to maintain order. Framed as a public health measure, the decree effectively granted the executive sweeping control over resources, prices, and security forces. It enabled the administration to deploy military and police power far beyond epidemiological needs, centralize decision-making, and suppress dissent under the justification of crisis management. In effect, Duterte's pandemic response blurred the line between health emergency and political consolidation.[7]

On March 23, 2020, UK Prime Minister Boris Johnson announced a nationwide stay-at-home order as COVID-19 spread rapidly. The UK Parliament passed the Coronavirus Bill, which granted the government sweeping emergency powers at a level unseen since World War II. Passed within days, it marked an extraordinary suspension of normal freedoms to protect public health and the NHS.,[89] Amid the pandemic, the government also launched its largest military investment in thirty years, framed as a response to new global threats.[10] Though justified as a move toward modernization and security, it also showed how crises can be used to redefine the boundaries of government authority.

In India, Prime Minister Narendra Modi's government used the pandemic to consolidate power and weaken democratic checks, accelerating what Heidelberg University professor Rahul Mukherji terms a slide toward "competitive authoritarianism." A nationwide lockdown was announced with just four hours' notice, no consultation with state government, and no deliberation in Parliament. Police curfews trapped millions of migrant workers far from home. Emergency governance was centralized under the opaque PM CARES fund. Opposition voices were sidelined, while the judiciary and bureaucracy deferred to the executive. Journalists and activists who reported on policy failures were charged with disseminating "fake news." Muslim communities, already politically vulnerable, were scapegoated as virus spreaders. What began as a public health crisis became a means to expand executive discretion and erode the country's federal fabric.[11]

Türkiye offers another example of how pandemic-era urgency was used to expand executive power and restrict civic space. In December 2020, Ankara passed the *Law on Preventing the Financing of the Proliferation of Weapons of Mass Destruction*, which was framed as a technical response to United Nations (UN) requirements. In practice, the law reached far beyond counterterrorism financing. The law granted the Interior Ministry broad power to audit, restrict, or suspend the activities of nongovernmental organizations; appoint state trustees to replace their elected leadership; halt fundraising; and freeze assets. Combined with selective prosecutions, limits on dissent, and intensified digital surveillance, Türkiye's pandemic response deepened the ongoing erosion of civil liberties. The government effectively used a global crisis to consolidate state control at a moment when public scrutiny was severely weakened.[12]

Sri Lanka followed a similar pattern. In early March, President Gotabaya Rajapaksa dissolved Parliament, and soon after the National Elections Commission postponed the April parliamentary elections indefinitely, citing the threat posed by the virus. As in India, the country's Muslim minority became a target of blame, accused of spreading COVID-19.[13]

Why Did Authoritarianism Increase? The growth of authoritarian tendencies during COVID-19 was not entirely unexpected. Throughout history, crises have often expanded government power as citizens become more willing to trade liberty for security. The pandemic created exactly such conditions. Faced with uncertainty and fear, many people accepted restrictions on movement, gatherings, privacy, and daily life that would have been difficult to imagine before 2020. The crisis also concentrated authority in executive institutions. Because most citizens lacked the expertise to assess epidemiological risks, governments and public-health agencies became the primary sources of information and decision-making. At the same time, modern surveillance technologies gave states unprecedented capacity to monitor compliance. History also suggests that emergency powers introduced during crises are not always fully reversed once the crisis passes, making temporary measures easier to normalize and institutionalize. Importantly, COVID-19 did not create authoritarian tendencies from nothing. In many countries, democratic backsliding was already underway. The pandemic often served as a catalyst, allowing leaders to expand powers they had long sought under the justification of emergency response. These were not isolated episodes. Around the world, the pandemic reshaped political authority at remarkable speed. From February 2020 to February 2022, 42 countries and territories have decided to postpone national elections and referendums.[14] V-Dem reports that 57 countries recorded moderate violations and a further 44 countries had major violations of international norms.[15] Emergencies have always tested institutional boundaries, but COVID-19 produced stress on a global scale. Some governments used the moment to centralize power, curtail civil liberties, or weaken independent oversight.

While many governments responded to the pandemic by centralizing authority, the United States produced the mirror image: a legislative revolt against executive emergency powers. According to a comprehensive review, more than 750 bills were introduced in state legislatures during 2020 and 2021, mostly aimed at restricting emergency powers, with at least 25 states enacting laws that curtailed the authority of governors or state health officials.[16]

Of course, not all countries moved toward greater state control. By 2022, countries such as New Zealand, Norway, and Sweden had removed most pandemic restrictions, while many jurisdictions, particularly in the United States, enacted laws limiting future emergency powers. Taken together, these reforms have quietly rewritten the legal architecture of public health and government reach in many parts of the world. In some countries, emergency powers expand the executive's reach; in others, such as across many U.S. states, legislatures moved to restrict them. What links these divergent paths is the long-term shift in how governments and societies understand emergency authority. Even if years pass without another outbreak, the effects of these changes will persist.

Beyond these legal challenges, broader democratic indicators also shifted during the pandemic. Freedom House, a global watchdog, rates countries on a 0–100 scale, with higher scores indicating greater political and civil freedoms. According to its 2025 data, 121 countries now have freedom scores below their pre-pandemic levels, while only 63 show any improvement. Overall, the global trends point to a measurable authoritarian shift, although the magnitude of these changes varied substantially across countries. In some states, emergency powers were rolled back after the crisis, while in others the pandemic accelerated longer-term trends toward centralized authority.

The pandemic did not only test hospitals, doctors, and public-health systems. It also tested governments and political institutions around the world. Faced with a rapidly spreading virus and enormous uncertainty, policymakers were forced to make difficult decisions involving public health, economic activity, education, civil liberties, and social stability. In many countries, emergency powers expanded, restrictions were imposed, and governments assumed responsibilities that would have been difficult to imagine only months earlier. Whether these measures were necessary or excessive remains a matter of debate. What is clear, however, is that COVID-19 demonstrated how quickly the relationship between citizens and the state can change during a crisis. It also revived a longstanding question in political science: when confronted with a challenge of this magnitude, which systems of government perform best?

Which Governance Proved to be Better?

Pandemics have political consequences, too. One aspect of political debate centers on which type of political regime proved more effective in containing the pandemic. This question arises in part because of a noticeable gap in reported death rates between democratic and undemocratic nations (or similarly free and non-free nations), with the former often reporting higher fatalities. The fatality rate in a democracy, at the end of the first year of the pandemic, is reported to be, on average, 3.7 times larger than in an autocracy.[17] Similarly, freer countries reported over 4 times more cases per million on average.[18] As a result, many argue that autocratic regimes may be more capable of swiftly implementing policies to curb the spread of COVID-19. For example, Slovenian philosopher Slavoj Žižek remarked "It seems that the strong approach to the crisis by the Chinese state has worked or at least worked much better than what is now occurring in Italy." He even recommended a new form of communism was needed to deal with the pandemic.[19]

On the other hand, several studies argue that this might be due to the underreporting of autocracies.[20] Recent research found that authoritarian regimes achieved lower COVID-19 infection and death rates than democracies when applying stringent policies, though issues of data transparency may partly explain this apparent advantage.[21]

Support for representative democracy has declined in many nations following the pandemic. A Pew survey suggests that, in 11 of the 22 countries with available data from 2017, the percentage of people who view representative democracy as a very good way to govern has dropped significantly. In both the UK and Canada, this share fell from 43% in 2017 to 31% in 2023. Similarly, in Sweden, it declined from 54% to 41% over the same period. At the same time, there is growing support for more authoritarian models of government.[22]

Notes

1. Camus and Gilbert (1991, p. 37)
2. https://assets.aclu.org/live/uploads/publications/asset_upload_file399_33642.pdf

3. Daniel (2024)
4. https://jamestown.org/buying-silence-the-price-of-internet-censorship-in-china/
5. https://www.washingtonpost.com/politics/2020/04/02/hungary-just-became-coronavirus-autocracy/
6. https://balkaninsight.com/2021/04/27/slovenian-protesters-rally-against-degradation-of-democracy/
7. https://apnews.com/article/virus-outbreak-leni-robredo-philippines-asia-east-asia-28b530198c4f86cd7e40675285d2f3a5
8. https://www.cnn.com/2020/03/23/uk/uk-coronavirus-lockdown-gbr-intl
9. https://coronavirus.blackstonechambers.com/coronavirus-and-civil-liberties-uk/
10. https://www.gov.uk/government/news/pm-to-announce-largest-military-investment-in-30-years
11. Mukherji (2020)
12. https://www.hrw.org/news/2020/12/24/turkey-draft-law-threatens-civil-society
13. Kahl and Wright (2021, p. 259)
14. https://www.idea.int/news-media/multimedia-reports/global-overview-covid-19-impact-elections
15. https://v-dem.net/documents/19/dr_2022_ipyOpLP.pdf
16. Davis et al. (2023)
17. Cassan and Van Steenvoort (2021); Sorci et al. (2020)
18. Erdem (2020b)
19. Zizek (2020, p. 65)
20. Cassan and Van Steenvoort (2021); Erdem (2020b)
21. Ha et al. (2024)
22. Pew Research Center (2024)

CHAPTER 8

Educationally Yours

Abstract This chapter analyzes the profound disruption to education systems caused by school closures and the rapid shift to online learning. It documents significant learning losses, especially among disadvantaged students, and argues that these effects may persist for years, shaping future labor markets and inequality. While acknowledging the acceleration of digital education tools, the chapter concludes that the overall impact on human capital formation has been largely negative and unevenly distributed.

Keywords Education • Learning loss • Remote learning • Inequality • Human capital • School closures

The pandemic has had an immense impact on education, maybe one of the hardest-hit parts of public life. Beginning in March 2020, schools all over the world shifted almost overnight to remote instruction, with no clear sense of when normalcy would return. Teachers had to improvise ways of creating new teaching materials and homework, while students faced a new kind of isolation where the line between home and school had blurred.

The main reason behind the school closure was to slow the spread of the virus. Public health officials said that the coronavirus spreads easily through close human contact, especially in indoor and crowded settings, which schools fit perfectly. Children, teachers, and staff could act as

O. Erdem, *The Socioeconomic Impact of Pandemics*,
https://doi.org/10.1007/978-3-032-24189-4_8

carriers even if they weren't severely ill, creating a hidden network of transmission.

More than a decade before COVID-19, researchers had already explored the consequences of sending children home during outbreaks. The problem with most of these studies is that it is very difficult, if not impossible, to isolate the effect of school closures from other interventions.

A very early and influential study advocating school closures was performed in 2006. The researchers imagined a small town and ran a simulation, showing that, because children and teenagers drive much of the spread, closing schools and keeping the young at home could suppress the transmission. It was among the first models to show how closing schools might work in the absence of vaccines.[1] Yet it remained just that, a simulation. It relied on strong assumptions and set aside economic and social disruptions. These models are useful as good baselines, but their results depend heavily on their premises. In this case, the model assigned children far more contacts than adults and also made them more infectious. Thus, if you change the assumptions, the conclusions would shift with them. Also, even if every assumption was perfectly accurate, they ignored the economic and social consequences of school closures, precisely the kinds of costs that loom so large in real pandemics and are central to the discussion in this book.

Later research turned to historical evidence to complement these early models. A study published in *The Lancet Infectious Diseases* in 2009 examines earlier cases and pandemics and again recognized how difficult it is to disentangle the impact of school closures from other interventions. Instead of relying on a single data set or model, they drew on several episodes where schools closed under different circumstances, such as the 1918 Spanish flu and the 1957 Asian flu, holidays in France, and even a teachers' strike in Israel. Each case is imperfect on its own; taken together, however, they help understand the possible effects of closures. Their review showed that the public imagination often exaggerated what school closures could accomplish. At best, closures can trim the total number of infections by roughly 15%, but their real strength lies elsewhere: they can sharply cut the transmission by as much as 40%, which can help hospitals survive the worst weeks. Yet these gains are fragile. If children simply gather elsewhere, which is very likely, the benefits evaporate. As the authors put it, authorities "must weigh the potential health benefits … against high economic and social costs, difficult ethical issues, and the possible disruption of key services such as health care."[2] The economic burden they outline is severe. In the UK, a 12-week closure could cost up to 1% of GDP; in the United States, estimates run as high as 6% of GDP. This is where I want to focus in this chapter. We cannot judge the efficiency of school closures without taking into consideration of their costs.

Another 2009 study concludes that U.S. strategies involving school closures are 14 to 21 times more costly than other single interventions.[3] Low-income families are hit hardest, losing access to school meals, reliable childcare, and stable income at exactly the moment a pandemic is most stressful. The authors' message is clear: "It is important to plan to mitigate the negative features of closure."[4] Thus, earlier studies generally supported school closures yet consistently underscored their significant costs. When COVID-19 struck, many of these theoretical concerns became reality.

Thus, the effectiveness of school closures cannot be evaluated in isolation; their impact on children, the economy, and broader social life must also be taken into account. For many children around the world, closures meant a prolonged interruption in education, raising the question of their long-run consequences. For example, according to one estimate global impact of school closures adds up to $15 trillion.[5]

So how did countries actually approach school closures? Political scientist Dr. Robert A. Maranto and his colleagues surveyed informants in 21 countries (the U.S., 15 European nations, Kazakhstan, Malaysia, and three developing countries: Colombia, Kenya, and South Africa) to capture how systems responded. Their respondents suggest that European countries, on average, moved more quickly to reopen physical schools and preserve academic continuity, while the U.S. tended to lean toward infection control and public anxiety management, even at the cost of learning loss and widening gaps.

They also noted that COVID deaths were overwhelmingly concentrated among the old and medically vulnerable: in California's first roughly 16,000 COVID deaths, only three were school-age children, and just 1.5% of deaths were under age 35.[6] In my interview with Dr. Maranto for this book, he noted that early in the pandemic, "we didn't know whether children were major vectors for the virus. But we knew by about May that kids didn't spread very much. We never adjusted policy to those facts."

Similarly, in early May, Italy reported around 200,000 infections, of which only about 2% involved children.[7] In April, the Royal Netherlands Institute of Public Health and the Environment (RIVM) stated in *The Brussels Times* that "children play a relatively small role in the spread of the virus."[8] Consistent with this assessment, Netherlands fully opened primary schools on June 8, 2020.

So, what happened was a policy inertia in many parts of the world: Even as evidence accumulated that children were not major spreaders, school systems in many parts of the world, including the United States, modeled their decisions on early fears rather than updated facts.

Dr. David Marshall, from the College of Education at Auburn University, argues in his book, *Lessons of the Pandemic* (co-authored with Dr. Tim Pressley from Christopher Newport University), that while the initial school closures in early 2020 were defensible due to limited information about COVID-19, the prolonged closures that followed were a grave policy mistake. Echoing the words of Robert Maranto, they contend that evidence from Europe, Southeast Asia, and early U.S. data from fall 2020 made clear that schools could have been reopened safely much sooner than they did. By mid-2020, mounting evidence from East Asia and Europe consistently showed that schools were not major vectors of transmission and that children faced milder medical risks than adults. In the authors' view, fear, politics, and bureaucratic inertia dictated the policy. The result was an educational crisis within a health crisis, one whose aftershocks will continue to be felt for a long time.[9]

These policy failures were compounded by the realities of remote learning. The sudden and unexpected shift to online learning during COVID-19 deepened the divide between students with advantages and those without. Those without reliable internet access or required technology fell behind their peers, while almost all lost their daily social interaction and peer learning. Even in a developed country like the UK, for example, when school closures were first implemented, it was reported that between 1.1 and 1.8 million children didn't have access to the internet or a laptop.[10] According to UNICEF, an organization responsible for providing humanitarian and developmental aid to children worldwide, approximately 463 million schoolchildren around the world lacked access to the internet, television, or radio. These children were left with virtually no means of continuing their education.[11]

In less developed countries, the situation was far more dire. *The Washington Post* reports how pandemic-era remote learning in Peru, where only one in three households had a computer at the time, sharply magnified existing inequalities. Wealthier students continued classes online with laptops and tutors, while poorer students relied on short TV lessons or shared phones. The dropout rates surged from 12% to 18%. Government efforts to distribute tablets and expand internet access fell short, revealing how COVID-19 turned education from a universal right into a privilege tied to wealth.[12]

In many countries, including the U.S., where schools serve daily meals, closures also disrupted meal programs that had long ensured breakfast and lunch to millions of children. This disproportionally affected the students from low-income families. The burden extended to families as well. Some families without nearby relatives or support felt obliged to remain at home with their kids, as there was no one else available to take care of their children.

The first U.S. test of remote learning began on March 5, when Washington's 24,000-student Northshore district closed schools and shifted online. Although some districts shut down earlier in response to local outbreaks, the nationwide wave of closures accelerated rapidly through March. By March 25, 2020, all of the states in the U.S. had closed all 100,000 public schools, thereby affecting almost 51 million students.[13] Nebraska and Maine were the final states to close their schools, doing so by April 2, 2020. From that point forward, schools across the country remained closed for the rest of the 2019–2020 academic year, marking the largest and most abrupt disruption to U.S. schooling in modern history.[14]

On the upside, schools and universities sought ways to adapt to online education. Many schools and colleges invested heavily in remote education tools and services that had rarely been used at scale before. While virtual teaching could not replicate exactly the richness of in-person learning, it reshaped the education industry for good. It fueled the growth of learning technologies, including artificial intelligence (see the following chapter, Technologically Yours, for details).

Reopening

Reopening, however, proved far more difficult than closing: Even though businesses and restaurants were reopened fairly quickly, within a couple of months in 2020, it took far longer for schools to do so. For many, this gap was puzzling: if society could reopen its shops and restaurants, why were classrooms kept closed?

By early May, schools had reopened in the Netherlands, Norway, Finland, France, Switzerland, Germany, and Spain.[15] By June 2020, more than 20 countries had resumed in-person schooling. Some, including

Sweden, Taiwan, and Nicaragua, never closed schools at all, creating a vast, informal global experiment.[16] At the beginning of the 2020–21 school year, four states in the U.S., Arkansas, Florida, Iowa, and Texas, mandated that in-person instruction be available for at least some grade levels. Although many schools resumed on-campus learning in limited forms, 74% of the nation's 100 largest school districts began the year using remote-only instruction, a decision that affected over nine million students nationwide.[17] Approximately half of public schools were still closed to in-person teaching by March 2021.[18]

Research shows that, especially in the United States, reopening decisions were shaped more by politics than by public health concerns. Republican-leaning districts reopened more frequently, and Democratic-leaning districts remained remote.[19]

The global picture was vastly mixed, but one thing was almost unique: the disadvantaged were harmed the most. In Chile, for example, reopening was highly unequal: affluent schools returned to in-person learning much earlier, while poorer schools remained closed far longer.[20]

Learning Loss

The consequences of these choices are now starkly visible. According to one measure, by the spring of 2022, American students had lost, on average, about half a year in math and a third of a year in reading. These losses were uneven: Districts with higher poverty, more minority students, and fewer resources saw larger declines.[21] Districts with high-poverty[22] schools that went remote experienced losses about 50 percent greater than low-poverty schools.[23] These setbacks deepened the preexisting inequities. Once again, the poor became poorer.

University of California professor Shamik Dasgupta describes school closures as a "moral catastrophe" and suggests that they did little to slow the pandemic but caused massive learning losses, especially for disadvantaged children. Although school closures were intended to slow transmission, their prolonged implementation led to precisely the negative consequences these researchers warned about. Moreover, the speed and the global scale of the closures forced the educators into an abrupt shift to online learning, often without preparation or infrastructure.

Economist Harry Patrinos, who worked 32 years at the World Bank as a senior education advisor and now leads the Department of Education Reform at the University of Arkansas, has been studying learning loss since

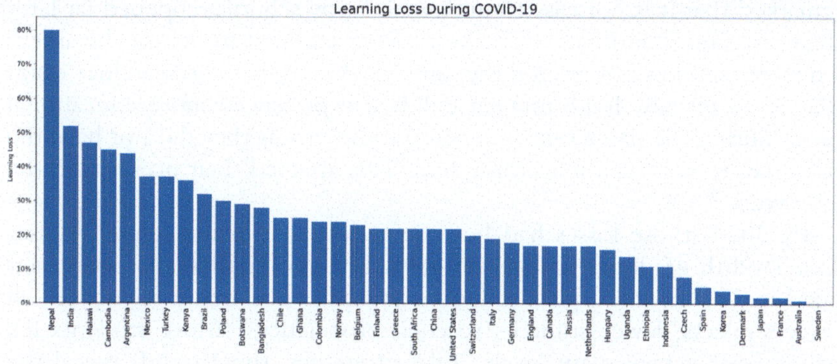

Fig. 8.1 Learning loss during COVID-19. Learning losses varied dramatically across the globe. Nepal experienced the deepest educational setbacks, while others, particularly more developed countries, managed to contain the damage to far lower levels. (Source: Prepared by Orhan Erdem using data from Patrinos [2023])

the start of the pandemic. He has recently examined the global educational fallout of COVID-19 across 41 countries. According to his calculations, the global average duration of closures was about 21 weeks, affecting more than 1.6 billion students, or 94% of the global student population. At one extreme, India's schools stayed closed for 93 weeks, and Bangladesh's for 63 weeks, while Sweden never closed its schools at all.[24] He also compiled loss estimates that other researchers had already calculated and then standardized them so that they could be compared. The associated learning losses are given in Fig. 8.1. According to this, countries like Nepal and India experienced some of the deepest educational setbacks, while others, particularly more developed countries, managed to contain the damage to far lower levels. It is worth mentioning that the learning loss of Sweden, which has never closed the preschools or elementary schools, is the lowest across these 41 countries.

He found a striking relationship: the longer schools stayed closed, the less children learned. Drawing on data from 41 countries, he estimated that each week of closure reduced learning by about 1% of the standard deviation, meaning that a 20-week shutdown amounted to losing nearly a full year of schooling. Crucially, Patrinos emphasizes that there is little evidence that school closures substantially reduced infection rates, yet the educational costs were immense.[25] In my interview with Dr. Patrinos, he remarked that it is not easy to understand why schools reopened far later than restaurants and bars: if the latter were assumed to be safe, he asked, why were schools not treated the same way? Also, many researchers claim that economically disadvantaged children experienced more educational losses during the pandemic, compared to others, as they did not have the resources to recover the learning loss. This affected their prospect in the later years.[26]

By 2024, those losses had become measurable in the United States, too: Twelfth-graders scored lower in reading and mathematics than their peers in 2019, while eighth-graders saw similar declines in science. In all three subjects, fewer students reached proficiency.[27] More students fell below basic achievement levels. Taken together, these trends reveal the pandemic's enduring educational scars. Almost everywhere in the world, there was an observable learning loss, with Sweden experiencing the least.

The OECD's Programme for International Student Assessment (PISA) provides one of the most commonly used international benchmarks of educational performance. Its 2022 report delivered a stark message: on average, mathematics scores across OECD countries fell by nearly 3% (15 points) and reading scores by about 2% (10 points) compared to PISA 2018, while science performance remained largely unchanged. In educational terms, this drop amounts to roughly three-quarters of a year of lost learning.

The OECD leaves little doubt about the source of the decline, attributing it to the shock effect of COVID-19 on most countries. As the report puts it,

> Across PISA-participating economies, at least half of students experienced COVID-related school closures for three months or more. Systems that spared more students from longer school closures scored higher while their students enjoyed a greater sense of belonging at school.[28]

Even the learning loss was not evenly distributed. Disadvantaged students, those from low-income households or minority families, bore the heaviest burden. As with so many other issues covered in this book, the pandemic's impact on education fell hardest on those who were already most vulnerable.

Notes

1. Glass et al. (2006)
2. Cauchemez et al. (2009)
3. Sander et al. (2009)
4. Cauchemez et al. (2009)
5. Psacharopoulos et al. (2021)
6. Maranto et al. (2023)
7. Zweig (2025, p. 64)
8. https://www.brusselstimes.com/107722/netherlands-wants-to-fully-open-primary-schools-before-the-summer
9. Marshall et al. (2024, Chapter 2)
10. https://www.telegraph.co.uk/women/life/national-education-union-putting-politics-pupils/
11. Ibid.
12. https://www.washingtonpost.com/world/2020/10/16/coronavirus-peru-remote-learning-inequality/
13. https://www.edweek.org/leadership/map-coronavirus-and-school-closures-in-2019-2020/2020/03
14. Marshall et al. (2024, Chapter 1)
15. Zweig (2025, p. 63)
16. https://www.science.org/content/article/school-openings-across-globe-suggest-ways-keep-coronavirus-bay-despite-outbreaks
17. https://www.americanprogress.org/article/remote-learning-school-reopenings-worked-didnt/
18. Macedo and Lee (2025, p. 131)
19. Hartney and Finger (2022)
20. Crato and Patrinos (2025, Chapter 2)
21. Kane and Reardon (2023)
22. They define a school as a “high-poverty” school if more than 75% of students received free and reduced-price lunch (FRPL).
23. Goldhaber et al. (2023)
24. Patrinos (2023)
25. Patrinos (2023)
26. Dasgupta (2022)
27. U.S. Department of Education (2025b, 2025c, 2025a)
28. OECD (2023)

CHAPTER 9

Technologically Yours

Abstract This chapter explores how the pandemic accelerated digital transformation and the adoption of artificial intelligence (AI). It argues that COVID-19 acted as a catalyst, pushing technologies such as remote work platforms, online education, and AI systems into mainstream use. While these developments increased efficiency and innovation, the chapter also highlights emerging risks, including ethical concerns, misinformation, and the widening digital divide, framing the pandemic as a turning point in technological evolution.

Keywords Technology • Artificial intelligence • Digital transformation • Innovation • Productivity • ChatGPT

Machines will be capable, within twenty years, of doing any work a man can do.
—Herbert Simon (1965), Nobel Prize-winning economist

Player Piano, a dystopian novel by the American author Kurt Vonnegut, was published in 1952, three years before the term "artificial intelligence [AI]" was first coined. Known for his satire and dark humor, Vonnegut imagined a future in which machines had largely replaced human jobs. The novel is set in the highly industrialized city of Ilium, where automation has displaced much of the workforce. First, muscle work was

O. Erdem, *The Socioeconomic Impact of Pandemics*,
https://doi.org/10.1007/978-3-032-24189-4_9

mechanized; then routine work; now even thinking is being automated. The protagonist, Dr. Paul Proteus, the son of a renowned engineer, follows in his father's footsteps and becomes one of the most successful managers at Ilium Works. Despite his privileged position within the technological elite, Paul grows increasingly disillusioned with the system and questions the human costs of a society organized around technological efficiency and automation.

Paul begins to sympathize with the struggles of the lower classes and eventually joins the Ghost Shirt Society, a rebellion group that resists the machine-driven hierarchy and views the unchecked power of the machines as lawlessness. According to the Ghost Shirt Society's leader, Lasher, machines are to humans what white men were to Native Americans. He believes that machines are destroying humanity, and one day humans will be servants of machines. The group opposes the mechanized society and seeks to restore human purpose and dignity through meaningful work. They believe that reclaiming humanity might require destroying at least some of the machines.

However, the rebellion ultimately fails, and Paul is captured and interrogated as one of the leaders of the Ghost Shirt Society. What Paul says during this interrogation highlights the novel's central critique, delivered as early as 1952, of the supremacy of the machines and dehumanizing effects of automation (Fig. 9.1).

Paul argues that true sovereignty in the U.S. belongs to the people, not to the machines. He said, "Machines and organization and pursuit of efficacy have robbed the American people of liberty and pursuit of happiness." Dismantling at least some of the machines, seemingly a regressive step, he argues, might actually be the step in the right direction. He added, "The main business of humanity is to do a good job of being human beings, … not to serve as appendages to machines, institutions, and systems."

The novel ends on a cynical note, "This isn't the end … Nothing ever is, nothing ever will be—not even the Judgement Day," reminding readers that the coexistence, and the struggle, between the humans and machines is likely to continue indefinitely. More than a half century after *Player Piano* was published, the same realization resurfaced in a different setting. In 2018, two years before the pandemic, Elon Musk, CEO of Tesla and, SpaceX, publicly admitted: "Yes, excessive automation at Tesla was a mistake. To be precise, my mistake. Humans are underrated."

Fig. 9.1 *Man and Machine*, Ida York Abelman, 1939. Public Domain. (Source: https://www.metmuseum.org/art/collection/search/360320)

The concept of AI is nothing new. Long before computers existed, humans imagined tools that could think, decide, or move on their own. Although not in the way we understand it today, it is argued that the concept of thinking machines dates back to ancient Greek mythology. Homer and Hesiod, for example, described self-moving and intelligent automatons crafted by Hephaestus, such as Talos, Pandora, and animated devices. These mythological creations have been interpreted as early representations of AI, underscoring their technological nature in ancient literature and art.[1]

The modern understanding of AI traces back to the late 1940s, as discussed in detail below. Yet for decades, these ideas and applications were largely confined to laboratories, universities, and specialized industries. It was COVID-19 pandemic that took AI into everyday life. The pandemic transformed it from abstract research agenda into a mass public technology. To understand how this moment became possible, it is useful to start with a brief history of artificial intelligence.

The Short History of Artificial Intelligence

In 1948, American mathematician Claude Shannon published a landmark paper that aimed to create a general mathematical framework for measuring how much information any source can produce and for sending it reliably over a noisy channel. Shannon showed that any message, whether text, photo, or data, can be broken into tiny yes/no "bits." His insights are now used in everything from next-word prediction in language models to modern data compression. To date, the paper has been cited more than 100,000 times.[2] Two years after this publication, in 1950, British mathematician and cryptanalyst Alan Turing published another breakthrough paper, "Computing Machinery and Intelligence," which begins with the provocative question, "Can machines think?"[3] Turing introduced the Turing test, which formed the fundamentals of understanding whether or not a computer or system has sentience. According to common understanding, if a system or computer passes the Turing test, it is conceived to have human intelligence. In other words, if a human interrogator cannot tell whether they are talking with a person or a computer, the machine is deemed to have passed the test.

In 1955, the American computer scientist and cognitive scientist John McCarthy coined the term "artificial intelligence (AI)" in a proposal for a summer research project at Dartmouth College. The project aimed to explore how machines could simulate human intelligence, including language use, problem-solving, and self-improvement. The term "artificial intelligence" was coined at this conference. Their practical definition was as follows: "For the present purpose, the artificial intelligence problem is taken to be that of making a machine behave in ways that would be called intelligent if a human were so behaving."[4] Thus, their conference defines AI as the attempt to build machines that replicate any aspect of human intelligence.

In 1957, psychologist Frank Rosenblatt created the Perceptron, an early computational model inspired by the human brain and widely referred as an introductory model for modern neural networks. The Perceptron demonstrated how machines could learn to classify information into two categories (e.g. short, long) by iteratively adjusting the model's internal parameters in response to data. This idea later become central to the machine learning. However, the original Perceptron was limited to single computational stage (layer), which meant it could not handle more complex problems.

A few years later, between 1964 and 1967, MIT professor Joseph Weizenbaum developed ELIZA, widely regarded as the first chatbot.[5] It worked by detecting keywords, and applying rule-based patterns, instead of machine learning, generating replies through prewritten templates without understanding the meaning. ELIZA pioneered human–computer dialogue and became an early program cited in discussions of the Turing test and machine intelligence.

Since the 1970s, neural networks have gone through repeated cycles of enthusiasm and skepticism.[6] A major turning point came in 1986, when the backpropagation algorithm developed by David Rumelhart and Ronald Williams at the University of California San Diego, together with Geoffrey Hinton at Carnegie-Mellon University, enabled the effective training of multi-layer networks. By allowing error signals to propagate backward through successive layers, backpropagation overcame the fundamental limitations of single-layer perceptrons and made it possible to learn complex settings. Although the method was conceptually powerful, it didn't end up creating a broad impact for many years due to insufficient computation power and limited access to large data sets.

Progress continued in small steps. In 1997, IBM's supercomputer Deep Blue beat the world chess champion, Garry Kasparov. The *New York Times* reported this with the headline "Swift and Slashing, Computer Topples Kasparov." This marked the first time a computer had ever defeated a human in a classical chess game. More than a decade later, in 2010, Apple introduced "Siri (Speech Interpretation and Recognition Interface)" and integrated it into iPhones. This marked a pivotal moment in the evolution of AI, as it brought voice-activated digital assistants into daily life. By combining speech recognition and natural language processing (NLP), Siri allowed millions of people to interact with their devices in a more human-like way.

The turning point came in 2012. At the University of Toronto, graduate students Alex Krizhevsky and Ilya Sutskever, working under the guidance of Geoffrey Hinton, decided to enter the ImageNet competition with a bold idea: training a deep neural network on graphics processors (GPUs), hardware originally designed for video games.[7] It turned out that these processors were well-suited for large-scale computation. Their system, which would become known as AlexNet, didn't just win, it crushed

Table 9.1 The Milestones of Artificial Intelligence

Milestone	*Year*
Claude Shannon's framework of information transmission	1948
Alan Turing's Turing test	1950
John McCarthy's Dartmouth Conference	1956
ELIZA, the first chatbot, developed by Joseph Weizenbaum	1967
Backpropagation enables multi-layer neural networks	1986
IBM's Deep Blue defeated Garry Kasparov, the world chess champion	1997
Apple introduces Siri, a voice-activated digital assistant	2010
Alex Krizhevsky's demonstrates the power of GPUs in deep learning	2012
OpenAI releases ChatGPT to the public	2022

the competition by a margin of 10.8%.[8] For the first time, computers could reliably recognize objects in images by learning directly from millions of examples.

Following this success, Krizhevsky joined Google, while Sutskever went on to co-found OpenAI.[9] In 2024, decades after its introduction, the significance of this contribution was formally recognized when Geoffrey Hinton was awarded the Nobel Prize in Physics (Table 9.1).

Artificial Intelligence Becomes Public

Despite these advances, widespread public engagement with artificial intelligence remained limited for decades. AI remained a field for specialists and enthusiasts, not yet part of everyday life. That dynamic changed dramatically in the aftermath of the COVID-19 pandemic. Although AI had been developed and used since the 1950s, the pandemic acted as a catalyst for its widespread adoption.

Global lockdowns forced people to stay at home, leading to a significant rise in internet usage. People who were confined to their homes turned to gaming, sought new ways to access services, and embraced online classes and videoconferencing. Hospitals, overwhelmed and searching for ways to streamline workflows, increasingly adopted digital tools and desperately looked for new ones. For example, a hospital in Washington State used a robot equipped with a camera, microphone, and stethoscope to treat the first person hospitalized in the U.S.[10] In China, Alibaba DAMO Academy and Alibaba Cloud developed AI-based imaging system capable of analyzing CT scans for suspected COVID-19 cases in just 20 seconds, achieving an accuracy rate of 96%. By comparison, physicians typically require 5 to 10 minutes to manually interpret a single patient's CT images. These innovations not only saved critical time for healthcare providers during a time when medical facilities were overwhelmed but also provided them with highly reliable diagnostic support.[11] As a result, the world suddenly became more dependent, and therefore more receptive, to these emerging digital and AI technologies.

This shift set the stage for a perfect moment for the widespread adoption of AI. In November 2022, OpenAI released ChatGPT, an AI-powered conversational tool that allowed users to pose questions and receive human-like responses. The time of its release aligned perfectly with a population newly accustomed to digital problem-solving and remote interaction. In a survey conducted by the World Economic Forum in 2020, 98% of respondents indicated they would like the option to work remotely for the remainder of their careers.[12]

The impact was immediate. Data from Google Trends, a tool that tracks the frequency of search terms over time, shows a sharp surge in queries for the term "artificial intelligence" beginning in November 2022, with interest climbing steadily since then (see Fig. 9.2). Public curiosity did not merely increase; it exploded.

ChatGPT's adoption was mind-blowing. In just 5 days, the number of ChatGPT users reached 1 million, soaring to 100 million within two months of its launch. According to the *Financial Times*, ChatGPT is the fastest-growing app ever, reaching 1 billion users in 3 years, much faster than either Google (which took 13 years) and Facebook (which took 8).[13] Now, as of 2025, it is estimated that 5.2 billion users visit chatgpt.com every month.[14] This explosive growth went beyond software. The stock value of NVIDIA, whose chips power much of OpenAI's infrastructure, surged tenfold in two years between October 2022 to October 2024.

Since its release, countless ChatGPT-like tools have emerged, such as Perplexity, Grok, Claude, and Gemini, quickly becoming part of daily life for students, teachers, researchers, and programmers alike. Tasks that once required substantial technical expertise are now accessible to anyone, and evidence shows that using these kinds of tools significantly boosts

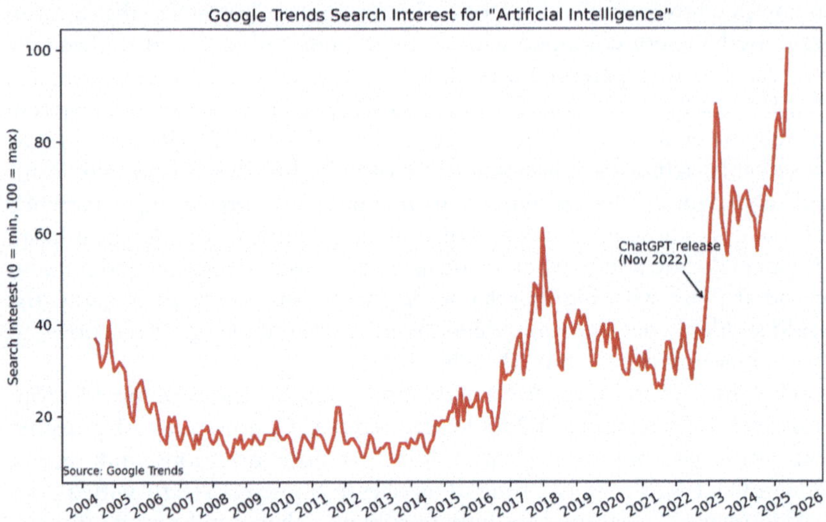

Fig. 9.2 Google Trends index for the search term "artificial intelligence" (June 2004–June 2025). Values are scaled, so the month with the greatest search volume equals 100. Interest waned through the late 2000s, began recovering in the mid-2010s, and surged after the public release of ChatGPT in November 2022, peaking in June 2025. (Source: Google Trends)

productivity in professional tasks.[15] An ordinary user can describe an idea and request a functional Python code for it. They can upload a lengthy PDF and receive a concise summary or ask for a clear explanation of a highly complex idea or theory. These tools can detect patterns in data, generate visualizations, and produce charts with a single prompt. Most of these tools, if not all, are available for free.

This surge in demand pushed the technology developers to improve and expand the existing tools, giving way to AI's new role. In their efforts to maintain operations, many businesses, especially in healthcare and education, turned to AI for support. AI played a critical role during the pandemic, especially in surveillance, diagnosis, and prediction. Many countries benefited from AI in analyzing social media data and Google searches to predict outbreaks, enhance early detection, resource allocation, and improve preparedness.[16] A Canadian company, Blue Dot, was among the first to flag the outbreak using AI to monitor news and travel data.

Infervision, a Chinese AI company, developed an algorithm to rapidly analyze lung CT scans, distinguish COVID-19 from other conditions, and reduce diagnostic times from 15 minutes to 10 seconds. Some other Chinese researchers developed a deep learning-based AI system trained on over 11,000 CT scans from more than 9000 patients, delivering results in under 3 seconds, almost 100 times faster than the average radiologist, who typically requires 6.5 minutes per case.[17] These are just a few among countless examples where AI enabled swift and efficient responses during the pandemic. In 2025, Google DeepMind became the first machine to achieve a gold medal at the 2025 International Mathematical Olympiad by solving 5 out of 6 problems entirely with no human intervention.[18] Such interventions drew global attention to the potential of AI. It boosted public trust and acceptance.

Unlike Deep Blue, which worked on rule-based environments like chess, ChatGPT does not require a fixed set of settings to work. And different from Siri, which primarily responds to voice commands, ChatGPT can reason and generate human-like text, and even produce speech across a wide spectrum of topics. Other chatbots can generate, and even convincingly replicate, human voices and videos. For example, voice synthesis tools developed by ElevenLabs can reproduce a person's voice with high precision using only a short audio sample. Similarly, video-generation platforms such as Synthesia can create realistic videos by combining text input with synthesized speech and digitally generated facial movements.

AI applications are increasingly embedded in everyday life in ways that are both practical and transformative. One striking example is Be My Eyes, an app originally designed to connect visually impaired users with AI or human volunteers through live video. The app can describe scenes, read text, identify objects, and answer contextual questions in real time.

Mustafa Suleyman, the CEO of Microsoft AI, calls this in his book, *The Coming Wave*, the "next great wave" of history.[19] According to Suleyman, the new wave is defined by two core technologies: artificial intelligence and synthetic biology, which are closely connected.

Advances in healthcare have also been numerous since COVID-19. Gene therapy, mRNA technology, and AI have significantly accelerated innovation in medicine. In 2021, researchers enabled a blind patient with retinitis pigmentosa, an eye disease that can lead to complete vision loss, to partially regain vision by using a gene therapy combined with specially engineered goggles. According to the researchers, "This is the first reported case of partial functional recovery" of vision restoration through this method.[20]

After ChatGPT's release in 2022, tech firms rushed to release their own AI models, each with its own strengths. Google unveiled Gemini, X announced Grok, Meta launched Llama, and Anthropic developed Claude, among others. Each model advances conversational AI in different directions, some emphasizing safety, others focusing on open access, real-time connectivity, or cultural tone. Elon Musk said, "AI is advancing vastly faster than any human." Investor enthusiasm has been equally remarkable. Reflecting the intense public and market demand for AI technologies, Anthropic confidentially filed for an initial public offering (IPO) with the U.S. Securities and Exchange Commission (SEC) in June 2026. The offering could become one of the most significant AI-related public offerings in history.

In June 2025, Microsoft released MAI-DxO, an AI-driven diagnostic model engineered for medical cases. Using more than 300 real-world cases published in the *New England Journal of Medicine (NEJM)*, the model, paired with OpenAI's o3, correctly identified the final diagnosis in 85 of the cases, compared with a 20% accuracy among human physicians. In addition, their model reportedly reduced diagnostic costs by 20%.[21]

A study has found that non-experts overwhelmingly prefer ChatGPT's medical advice over that of physicians, when they don't know the source of the responses.[22] Experts have the same opinion, too. In a study, a group of researchers posed health questions from Reddit's r/AskDocs to both physicians and the AI chatbot (ChatGPT). A panel of licensed healthcare professionals, blinded to which response came from the chatbot or a physician, evaluated 195 question-response pairs. They preferred ChatGPT's answers 79% of the time, rating them significantly higher for empathy.[23]

As AI innovation accelerates, the entire world is being reshaped in real time. On one side, it provides once-unimaginable benefits, like curing diseases, speeding up many processes like coding, and unlocking new scientific insights. On the other side, it poses some concerns and risks, such as job displacement, ethical dilemmas, and security threats.

The Risks of Artificial Intelligence

As with all technological advances, artificial intelligence did not come risk-free. Among the issues that concern scientists are deepfakes, bias and hallucination. Because AI models are trained on human-generated data such as conversations, videos, and written texts, modern systems can now convincingly replicate human voices and even produce realistic videos. This capability can be exploited for malicious purposes, a phenomenon which is commonly referred to as deepfake technology. In one case, criminals successfully impersonated as a senior executive and convinced the CEO of a UK-based company to transfer €220,000 (~$243,000) during a phone call.[24] The voice was so convincing that it reproduced the executive's accent and speech patterns, illustrating how AI can exploit human trust.

Also, AI models are prone to making the same cognitive and social biases found in their training data. For example, when asked to draw a medical doctor, they tend to pick a white male over other combinations.[25] In one experiment, a researcher asked an AI to draw "Black African doctors providing care for white suffering children." Instead, the system reportedly portrayed the children as Black, and sometimes depicted the doctors as white, contradicting the instructions.[26] These distortions are not random issues. They reveal how these models absorb and reproduce statistical patterns in their data, which are mostly produced by humans. Thus, they replicate human biases.

The other issue is known as "hallucination," which is defined as confidently fabricating information that is not factual. In one experiment, we asked various large language models (LLMs) to provide us with references in specific financial settings. The results revealed that 20% of the output we received from GPT-4o, 21% from o1-preview, and 77% from Gemini Advanced were fabricated.[27] The danger is not theoretical. In a stunning incident, lawyer Steven Schwartz submitted a legal brief citing six cases to a New York court, only to realize that they were all fabricated by ChatGPT, which he had relied on without verification.[28]

These models can produce nonexistent Bible verses, academic articles that were never written, or reference books that have never been published. Their responses may appear confident, polished, even smart, yet parts of it can be entirely imaginary. Users, therefore, must treat AI-generated output with both enthusiasm and skepticism and should verify it before using.

Together, bias and hallucination form a troubling pair. One amplifies the inequalities of the past; the other creates new errors.

Artificial intelligence also poses some risks for the job market. According to the Federal Reserve Bank of New York's February 2025 release, computer science and computer engineering, two of the most popular majors, are among the ten majors with the highest unemployment rates. This might be because AI models' coding skills are extremely accurate.

There are also more serious, existential threats. Researchers and industry leaders point out malicious use of AIs, such as engineering new viruses to create new pandemics, or developing autonomous weapons. AI chatbots can provide instructions to anyone to develop dangerous biological tools. The Center for AI Safety, a nonprofit organization working on reducing the social risks of AI, reports that the cost of gene synthesis, which can be used to create new hazardous biological agents, has been halving every 15 months.[29] Reflecting these fears, many public figures, researchers, CEOs, and professors from various universities from all over the world signed a statement in 2023 stating, "Mitigating the risk of extinction from AI should be a global priority alongside other societal-scale risks such as pandemics and nuclear war."[30]

On the social side, AI might be used to spread propaganda, surveillance, or deception. As increasing numbers of people rely on AI-powered chatbots such as ChatGPT, they may become vulnerable to misinformation, whether generated intentionally or unintentionally by these systems. Every day, chatbots learn more about our emails, intentions, and planned actions. Imagine that, one day, governments use chatbots for surveillance, which might be the easiest way to control the masses. Most of the largest chatbots, and, more broadly, the technology, are controlled by the biggest corporations and a few elites in the world. As these systems learn and consume more data about people, they could implement large-scale power over the public, and even an unintended form of mass control. Historically, technology has not always benefited society.

Will Artificial Intelligence Take Our Jobs?

The answer to this question is both yes and no. AI does not transform the labor market evenly. It will alter some occupations while leaving others largely the same. In many cases, AI does not eliminate jobs outright but changes what it takes to perform them. Tasks that once required modest training now demand greater expertise, effectively raising the bar for entry. At the same time, roles built around routine and repetitive work, such as basic data entry or text-writing, are especially vulnerable, as these tasks can be automated with relative ease.

Empirical evidence supports this uneven impact. One paper published in 2025 shows a sharp decline in employment among 22–25-year-olds in AI-exposed occupations such as software development and customer service following the adoption of generative AI tools, while older workers in the same fields were largely unaffected.[31] The pattern suggests not a widespread job destruction, but a gradual disappearance of entry-level positions.

At the same time *The Economist* argues that, so far, AI has reshaped white-collar work more than it has destroyed it.[32] White-collar jobs, broadly defined as professional, managerial, administrative, and office-based roles that rely primarily on cognitive rather than manual labor, have continued to expand in both employment and real wages in the United States since 2022. Growth has been strongest in positions that combine technical expertise with human judgment and coordination, such as project management, data-driven analysis, and supervisory roles. By contrast, employment declines have been concentrated on routine back-office functions, where tasks are repetitive, rules-based, and therefore easier to automate, such as text generation, coding tasks, retrieval of information, transcription, and translation.

Much like the pandemic itself, AI has been reshuffling the labor market rather than wiping it out. It is changing which skills matter, how work is organized, and who gains access to opportunity.

Economists Daron Acemoglu and Simon Johnson, both from the Massachusetts Institute of Technology (MIT), argue, in their book *Power and Progress*, that technological progress does not always lead to a shared prosperity across society. For example, they say that from 1980 on, even though the average productivity increased by over 1.5%, largely due to technological improvements, the median real wages (hourly compensation) increased by only 0.45%. This was not the case between 1949 and 1973, during which the increased productivity was closely aligned with an equally rising real wage.[33]

Similarly, MIT economists David Autor and Neil Thompson emphasize that not all jobs will be affected in the same way. Their research showed that what matters most is how much expertise a job requires, not just how many tasks it involves. Thus, an engineer will not be affected in the same way as the inventory clerk. When AI makes jobs need more expertise, wages tend to go up but fewer people can do those jobs, so employment goes down. By contrast, when AI makes jobs need less expertise, more people can do them, which increases employment but pushes wages down. In other words, jobs that need less expertise are at higher risk from automation; jobs that demand more expertise are not only safer but will probably see wage increases.[34]

Will AI take over? The pandemic is over. Although corporations, universities, and institutions have been using AI since the 1950s, for years it mostly remained a "behind-the-scenes" technology. Lockdowns during COVID-19 forced corporations to find solutions which did not require human labor. People looked for ways to do their jobs without their colleagues, and students embraced digital learning platforms. Chatbots like ChatGPT allowed anyone with internet access to leverage AI for everyday tasks, from writing emails to designing code. Thus, the public all over the world became vulnerable to the perils and promises of AI-driven productivity overnight. On the bright side, it increased everyone's productivity from education to scientific developments, by generating new information. On the downside, AI can easily be used for malicious purposes, from designing biological weapons to generating convincing fake videos. Concentrated in the hands of a few, it might turn into a mass surveillance system, potentially harming and destroying individual freedom and democracy.

However, one of its offspring, the resurgence of AI, is here to stay with all its perils and promises. This AI aftershock leaves society with a dual mandate. First, we must harness AI's potential, from discovering new medicines to developing more personalized education improving human expertise. Second, we need diligent regulations so that it does not harm humanity. We should not let AI control humanity. Civic society must act to force the authorities to develop rules to safely govern AI. In other words, we must unlock AI's benefits and craft regulations that keep it under control at the same time.

Crisis as Catalyst

From the abstract ideas of the 1950s to the deep-learning breakthroughs of recent decades, artificial intelligence evolved slowly and largely out of public view. For much of its history, AI remained an impressive technology, powerful and yet distant from everyday life. The COVID-19 pandemic changed that trajectory. Lockdowns, overwhelmed healthcare systems, remote work, and online education created an environment in which AI was no longer optional but necessary. When conversational systems (chatbots) emerged at this moment, they encountered a global population ready to rely on these digital tools. Almost overnight, AI shifted from a niche technology reserved for experts into public utility.

This transition marks a historical turning point. AI is no longer merely a subject of research papers or corporate infrastructure; it has become a social force that shapes how people work, learn, communicate, and make decisions. With this rapid shift comes a profound dilemma. On one side, AI offers extraordinary gains in productivity. On the other side it amplifies bias, fabricates false information, and raises deep ethical and political concerns. As with earlier technological revolutions, the question is not whether AI will change the society, but how that change will be governed. The pandemic did not create AI, but it pushed humanity abruptly into a new era, one for which our institutions, norms, and safeguards were only partially prepared.

Notes

1. Mayor (2023)
2. Shannon (1948)
3. Turing (1950)
4. McCarthy et al. (1955)
5. Weizenbaum (1966)
6. Narayanan and Kapoor (2024, p. 108)
7. Krizhevsky et al. (2012)
8. https://qz.com/1307091/the-inside-story-of-how-ai-got-good-enough-to-dominate-silicon-valley
9. Narayanan and Kapoor (2024)
10. https://www.theguardian.com/us-news/2020/jan/22/coronavirus-doctors-use-robot-to-treat-first-known-us-patient
11. Ding et al. (2025)
12. Coronavirus: Is working from home working? | World Economic Forum
13. https://www.ft.com/content/6df0a725-15bf-4bab-ace5-e3cafdb21542
14. https://www.semrush.com/website/chatgpt.com/overview/
15. Noy and Zhang (2023)
16. Arora et al. (2021); Hussain et al. (2024)
17. Jin et al. (2020)
18. https://www.nytimes.com/2025/07/21/technology/google-ai-international-mathematics-olympiad.html
19. Suleyman and Bhaskar (2023)
20. Sahel et al. (2021)
21. Nori et al. (2025)
22. Ozdemir et al. (2024)
23. Ayers et al. (2023)
24. https://www.wsj.com/articles/fraudsters-use-ai-to-mimic-ceos-voice-in-unusual-cybercrime-case-11567157402

25. https://www.bloomberg.com/graphics/2023-generative-ai-bias/, Rendering misrepresentation: Diversity failures in AI image generation | Brookings
26. https://www.npr.org/sections/goatsandsoda/2023/10/06/1201840678/ai-was-asked-to-create-images-of-black-african-docs-treating-white-kids-howd-it-
27. Erdem et al. (2025)
28. Weiser and Schweber (2023)
29. Hendrycks et al. (2023)
30. https://safe.ai/work/statement-on-ai-risk
31. Brynjolfsson et al. (2025)
32. https://www.economist.com/finance-and-economics/2026/01/26/why-ai-wont-wipe-out-white-collar-jobs
33. Acemoglu and Johnson (2023, p. 256)
34. Autor and Thompson (2025)

CHAPTER 10

Socially Yours

Abstract This chapter examines the social and cultural consequences of the pandemic, including mental health crises, changing family dynamics, and shifts in social behavior. It highlights the rise in isolation, domestic violence, and substance abuse, alongside changes in crime patterns and community interactions. The chapter also explores how the pandemic influenced spirituality, social cohesion, and the structure of everyday life, arguing that COVID-19 fundamentally reshaped how individuals relate to each other and to society.

Keywords Social impact • Mental health • Behavior • Community • Societal change

So far, I have covered several dimensions of COVID-19's impact on our lives. Yet its social reach extended even further, reshaping how people behaved in public, how they lived in private, and how, as a community, they searched for connection and meaning. COVID-19 did more than disrupt routines; it reshaped the basic structure of social life. Public spaces emptied, private spaces intensified, and the boundaries between the two blurred. In effect, the pandemic created a world where life became more interior and unequal.[1] This chapter briefly touches on some of these social

O. Erdem, *The Socioeconomic Impact of Pandemics*,
https://doi.org/10.1007/978-3-032-24189-4_10

and cultural consequences, which emerged from this shift in how people lived, connected, and endured.

Crime

As cities around the world became unusually quiet, the nature of crime changed. Most outdoor crimes decreased. Once stay-at-home rules took effect, crime levels collapsed almost overnight in major cities. Overall crime fell by roughly one-third, with the sharpest drops in offences that feed on crowds and movement: theft and robbery fell by nearly half, while assaults, burglaries, and vehicle thefts also declined.[2]

But the picture was not uniform. Homicide was the major exception. In many cities around the world, murder rates did not fall at all. In the United States, they rose dramatically. Between 2019 and 2020, the murder rate jumped from 6 to 7.6 per 100,000 people, the largest single-year increase since national data collection began. The rise continued in 2021 and 2022. Even as late as 2023, it remained above pre-pandemic levels.[3]

The overall decline in crime created a distorted picture of safety, because the very conditions that emptied the streets also heightened risks inside the home. Police departments and social-service agencies began reporting rises in domestic violence. The pandemic did not eliminate crime; it relocated it.

The surge in domestic violence during COVID-19 was one of the most disturbing social consequences of the pandemic. Several factors drove this increase. Lockdowns confined victims and abusers under the same roof for extended periods. Time spent at home surged. At the same time, economic stress, driven by job losses and decreasing income, intensified household tensions. Alcohol consumption rose in many countries. Worse still, support services, such as shelters, counseling centers, and courts, were either closed or worked with limited hours.

Hayley Foster, the chief executive of Women's Safety New South Wales (Australia) and a veteran advocate with 15 years supporting victims of domestic violence, described 2020 as the worst year the sector has ever witnessed.[4]

Similar patterns emerged across continents: In Peru, authorities observed an increase in disappearances of women and a rise in gender violence, consistent with global trends. In West Africa, historian Toby Green, drawing on interviews across Angola and Cape Verde, reports that lockdowns led to a sharp increase in teenage pregnancies. Deprived of stable jobs, many young women were forced into prostitution to survive.[5]

The Mind Under Pressure

What unfolded inside households was only one part of a larger problem. The pandemic strained people's inner lives as much as it disrupted cities. It pulled millions into new forms of anxiety, loneliness, and exhaustion. A term that suddenly entered everyday conversation was *burnout*, used to describe the sense of depletion and reduced motivation at work.

Government-ordered lockdowns, quarantines, and stay-at-home orders left many people isolated, and loneliness often gave way to anxiety, depression, and other mental health struggles. Research confirms that epidemics, including COVID-19, consistently lead to increases in psychiatric disorders such as depression, anxiety, post-traumatic stress disorders, and sleep problems.

A global review of studies found that during COVID-19, roughly one in five people (21%) experienced probable anxiety, nearly one in six (18%) probable depression, and about one in eight (13%) significant psychological stress, all higher than pre-pandemic levels.[6]

Young people suffered acutely. A nationwide survey by The Prince's Trust conducted in early 2021 in the UK revealed that one in four Britons aged 16 to 25 felt "unable to cope with life" during lockdowns. Half reported that their mental health had worsened since the pandemic began, and more than half said they either "always" or "often" felt anxious.[7] In England, the proportion of children experiencing a mental disorder rose sharply during the pandemic years. Among boys, rates increased from 11% in 2017 to 17% in 2020, while among girls, they climbed from 10% to 15%.

This escalation reflects the profound psychological toll of COVID-19 restrictions on younger generations and their emotional well-being.[8] A generation absorbed a psychological shock that will likely echo for years.

Mental health was not the only hidden consequence. Fear of infection also reshaped people's healthcare routines. Because of their fear of catching the COVID-19 virus in hospitals, many people also delayed or avoided critical care, such as cancer screening, involving mammograms, colonoscopies, and prostate exams. In April 2020, the number of screenings in the United States dropped by nearly 90% compared to normal levels, and ER visits dropped by 42%.[9]

When fear remained longer than the virus itself, people reached not only doctors and therapists but also for spiritual support.

Religious Services

> The catastrophe was so overwhelming that men, not knowing what would happen next to them, became indifferent to every rule of religion or law.
> —Thucydides, 460–400 BC.

In Camus's *The Plague*, churches fill with worshippers during the plague times, as sermons have become collective rituals. The gatherings have given people a sense of belonging at a time when the city of Oran's gates are closed, trade has collapsed, and families are separated. Crises often push people toward faith, and COVID-19 was no exception.

History offers stark reminders of this tension. During the Spanish flu, even though authorities strongly urged people to practice social distancing, as we had during COVID-19, Bishop Antonio Álvaro y Ballano, from the Spanish city of Zamora, called on his congregation to gather for nine consecutive days of prayer (a novena) in the church and continued to hold daily masses. According to the bishop, the pandemic was caused by "sins and ingratitude." In the end, Zamora recorded the highest death rate of any city in Spain, more than 10 times that of Madrid and 5 times the Spanish average.[10] Yet far from being accountable for his reckless behavior, Álvaro y Ballano was even rewarded in recognition of his heroic efforts during the pandemic.[11] His defiance became a tragic symbol of faith colliding with scientific reality.

A century later, during the early months of COVID-19, most religious buildings were closed. Yet, as Camus anticipated, people felt an even greater need for spiritual connection. Thus, they turned to livestreamed Zoom services and other forms of virtual prayer groups. In the United States, the word "prayer" became one of the most searched words on Google.

Yet after the initial phase of the pandemic, the general trend of attending religious services declined. Between 2016 and 2019, an average of 34% of U.S. adults reported attending services weekly. That figure fell to 30% between 2021 and 2023.[12]

While COVID-19 clearly disrupted worship practices, this decline likely reflects a broader, ongoing trend of secularization that predates the pandemic.

Those Pushed Furthest to the Margins

As the strain of the pandemic was felt everywhere in daily life, people searched for steadiness wherever they could find it: in virtual communities, in faith, or quiet routines that made days feel less uncertain. But not everyone had equal access to these forms of support. For some groups, especially those already living out of social visibility, the crisis magnified vulnerabilities that had long existed. And no group felt this more acutely than the elderly.

Think back to Margaret Keenan, the 90-year-old grandmother mentioned earlier, who received the first COVID-19 vaccine in the world. The moment she was vaccinated, she had said she could finally look forward to spending time with her family again after being alone for most of the year. Her relief captured what millions of older people could not so easily put into words.

In many countries, visits to nursing homes and care facilities were strictly prohibited, isolating those who were already among the most vulnerable. It is understandable that policymakers acted to shield the elderly residents from being infected, given their higher risk. However, these policies often failed to account for the severe psychological and cognitive costs of prolonged isolation. What was intended as protection from infection often became a form of confinement. Deprived of regular contact with family and friends, many residents ended up with loneliness and cognitive decline.

A 2023 meta-analysis published in *Ageing Research Reviews* examined the effects of COVID-19-related social isolation on older adults' cognitive function and mental health across 32 studies from 18 countries. The researchers found that more than half of older adults with dementia experienced worsening cognitive impairment, and nearly half developed new or aggravated behavioral symptoms. Among older adults without dementia, about one in four reported subjective cognitive decline, and 30% experienced worsening mental health, particularly depression.[13]

Looking back from 2025, Daniel Koch, who led the communicable diseases division at Switzerland's Federal Office of Public Health in 2020, reflected:

> We certainly didn't react well when it came to retirement homes. We issued recommendations that, I have to say, went too far. … People were locked in without being asked whether or not they wanted to be.[14]

Total isolation was a blunt instrument, chosen out of fear and uncertainty when more nuanced strategies might have balanced safety with dignity. Controlled precautions, such as limited, distanced visits with proper protective measures, outdoor meetings, or regular testing of visitors, were feasible. Some countries eventually adopted them. In the early months, however, policymakers often treated older adults as fragile objects to be shielded, rather than as individuals capable of assessing risk and expressing preference. In hindsight, the pandemic revealed not only how unprepared our health systems were, but also how paternalistic our approach to aging had become. Protecting life should never have meant suspending the humanity of those we sought to save.

Coping Through Substance Use

A 2022 *JAMA* study revealed a striking 25% rise in alcohol-related deaths in the United States during the first year of the COVID-19 pandemic. The sharpest increases occurred among adults aged 25–44, and deaths linked to both alcohol and synthetic opioids surged by nearly 60%.[15]

Drug overdoses followed a similar trajectory. Across several U.S. states, overdose deaths rose by 9–50%, and in Ontario, Canada, by 38% during the first months of the pandemic. San Francisco experienced a 55% increase in opioid deaths.[16] The pandemic intensified an already severe overdose crisis.

Not all of the consequences of the pandemic were felt immediately. Some emerged gradually, and some will continue to appear in time. Researchers from Singapore conducted a review of a vast amount of studies conducted across 49 countries. They focused on how COVID-19 physical distancing measures affected 11 vulnerable groups, including children, older adults, low-income populations, migrants, prisoners, people with disabilities, and minorities. Their review reveals widespread unintended harms such as loneliness, mental distress, job and income loss, food insecurity, disrupted education, and reduced access to healthcare and social services. Overall, they conclude that distancing measures, while effective in limiting viral spread, exacerbated existing inequalities and vulnerabilities.[17]

Time and again, across nearly every measure, it is apparent that COVID-19 disproportionately harmed those who were already disadvantaged. This exacerbated the gap between the advantaged and disadvantaged.

Notes

1. The disappearance of crowds didn't just quiet city streets; it also changed what happened inside big public spaces like stadiums. College football teams lost their home-field advantage as crowds were absent, revealing that it's crowd noise, rather than mere presence, that unsettles visiting teams. The usual home-team advantage largely disappeared in 2020.
2. Nivette et al. (2021)
3. https://www.cdc.gov/nchs/state-stats/deaths/homicide.html
4. https://www.theguardian.com/society/2020/dec/01/the-worst-year-domestic-violence-soars-in-australia-during-covid-19
5. Green (2021, p. 164)
6. Leung et al. (2022)
7. https://www.telegraph.co.uk/news/2021/01/19/one-four-young-people-feeling-unable-cope-lockdown-takes-toll/
8. https://www.telegraph.co.uk/news/2021/01/12/third-lockdown-has-triggered-unprecedented-crisis-mental-health/
9. Chen et al. (2021); Hartnett et al. (2020); Shukla et al. (2022)
10. Mulet (2019)
11. Spinney (2017, p. 83)
12. U.S. Church Attendance Still Lower Than Pre-Pandemic and Church Attendance Has Declined in Most U.S. Religious Groups
13. Prommas et al. (2023)
14. https://www.swissinfo.ch/eng/demographics/covid-19-daniel-koch-recalls-the-role-of-the-federal-council/89017839
15. White et al. (2022)
16. Imtiaz et al. (2021)
17. Li et al. (2023)

EPILOGUE

Do not act as if you were going to live ten thousand years.Death hangs over you.While you live, while it is in your power, be good.

—Marcus Aurelius, Roman Emperor, philosopher, 121–180 AD

Every decision we make carries a trade-off; gaining one thing means giving up another. Going to school costs free time and working long hours costs rest. There is no such thing as a riskless choice. This is one of the principles of economic reasoning. The pandemic was no exception.

Lockdowns and school closures were collective decisions, each involving a balance between saving lives and absorbing social and economic costs. At one extreme, closing everything forever would have prevented viral spread, but halted all economic activity. At the other extreme, keeping everything open would have allowed rapid transmission and resulted in far more deaths than the world experienced. In practice, countries chose very different points along this spectrum, producing remarkable variation in pandemic responses. COVID-19 will not be the last pandemic humanity faces.

Although stringent policies imposed substantial fiscal costs on governments, and significant social disruption, they were often defended by appeals to healthcare systems and savings lives. China, for example, repeatedly declared that it placed lives above economic growth.[1] That's why their approach was to focus on healthcare only. Global public opinion

O. Erdem, *The Socioeconomic Impact of Pandemics*,
https://doi.org/10.1007/978-3-032-24189-4

initially aligned with this framing. In April 2020, nearly three-quarters of the British, about 60% of Americans, and Japanese respondents, and almost 55% of the Germans believed that the government's top priority should be to limit the spread of the disease and reduce deaths, even if doing so risked a major recession, depression, and job losses.[2] In all of these countries, it took more than a year for public support to shift substantially, with these shares declining to around 40% only by September 2021.

Not all countries viewed this trade-off in the same way. Greater concern about the economic consequences was more predominant in Eastern Europe. Bulgaria, Hungary, Poland, Slovenia, Czechia and Italy, indicated that they believed the economic damage outweighed the potential health benefits.[3] In an atmosphere of heightened alarm, fear, and emergency, public dissent against the "at-all-costs" approach remained limited in many places. Critical voices were sidelined, and the belief that the containment of the virus must be performed regardless of the cost became dominant. As a result, most governments mandated extensive non-pharmaceutical interventions.

First lesion of the pandemic is that trade-offs do not disappear in crises. These measures, however, could not be evaluated solely by their intended benefits. Every policy carries costs, and pandemic responses were no exception. What I argued in this book is not public health interventions are unnecessary. On the contrary, many were essential. The failure lay elsewhere.

Effective crisis management requires clearly defined guidelines and continuous reassessment, not ad hoc improvisation. Although most of the developed countries possessed analytical as well as economic tools to assess trade-offs, political incentives and populist pressures frequently shaped decisions more than cost–benefit analysis. Many actions taken were not those that maximized social welfare, but those that minimized the public anger, largely derived from fear and uncertainty.

Second, every major crisis disproportionately hurts the most disadvantaged members of our society, and COVID-19 was no exception. By "disadvantaged," I refer to individuals with limited political influence or connections, low-income individuals, those with lower levels of education, and minorities. The costs of recovery or containment responses fell disproportionately on these groups.

Millions of children experienced substantial educational losses resulting from prolonged school closures, particularly those who were already lagging behind, or lacked adequate remote learning infrastructure. Thousands of small businesses disappeared permanently, leading to widespread job losses. Essential workers, meanwhile, were often insufficiently protected, in terms of both health risks and income security. Prolonged measures protected many, but they also shifted costs onto those least able to bear them. Thus, inequality deepened: the poor get poorer, the rich grow richer, and social divisions intensified.

Again, this does not imply that decisive action was a mistake. The failure of stringent measures was not the willingness to act, but failure to adapt. As evidence emerged (that these measures were harming disadvantaged), policies should have been updated.

Third, no single political action should be implemented solely based on its benefits; every policy carries costs. The pandemic response imposed substantial costs on the education of the younger generation and created generational debt, to name just a few. Did the benefits outweigh these costs? In this book, I argue that, for much of the world, the answer was largely no, as early decisions were not updated as evidence emerged.

The purpose of this book is not to blame anyone, but to inform future responses. It is very possible that we would have COVID-19-like pandemics again. My hope is that this book serves a broad audience, from economic agents, to educators, parents, and policymakers, as a reminder that there is always an optimum balance point, we should seek when responding to pandemics. Policies should not be evaluated and implemented solely by their intended benefits, but assessed in light of their full economic, social, and human costs.

In his novel *Blindness,* the Portuguese author José Saramago, Nobel Laureate in Literature, suggests that fear can make people blind. I would twist this slightly: emergencies can also cause blindness, and blindness often leads to poor judgment. What we must not repeat is allowing the emergency to blur our vision of trade-offs. Crises do not eliminate costs; they push them into shadows, often onto those who are least able to bear them. If future pandemics arrive, we must resist the temptation to treat emergencies or fear as a policy framework. When urgency replaces judgment, the bill eventually comes due, with interest.

Notes

1. http://english.scio.gov.cn/whitepapers/2020-06/07/content_76135269_5.htm
2. kekst-cnc_research-report_covid19_opinion-tracker_wave-9_october2021.pdf
3. https://www.europarl.europa.eu/at-your-service/files/be-heard/eurobarometer/2020/public_opinion_in_the_eu_in_time_of_coronavirus_crisis/report/en-covid19-survey-report.pdf

References

Acemoglu, D., & Johnson, S. (2023). *Power and progress: Our thousand-year struggle over technology and prosperity*. PublicAffairs.

Aiello, A. E., Perez, V., Coulborn, R. M., Davis, B. M., Uddin, M., & Monto, A. S. (2012). Facemasks, hand hygiene, and influenza among young adults: A randomized intervention trial. *PLoS One, 7*(1), e29744. https://doi.org/10.1371/journal.pone.0029744

Aladangady, A., Chang, A. C., & Krimmel, J. (2023). Greater wealth, greater uncertainty: Changes in racial inequality in the survey of consumer finances. *FEDS Notes* (2023-10-18–2), None-None. https://doi.org/10.17016/2380-7172.3405.

Almond, D. (2006). Is the 1918 influenza pandemic over? Long-term effects of *In Utero* influenza exposure in the post-1940 U.S. population. *Journal of Political Economy, 114*(4), 672–712. https://doi.org/10.1086/507154

Alwan, N. A., Burgess, R. A., Ashworth, S., Beale, R., Bhadelia, N., Bogaert, D., Dowd, J., Eckerle, I., Goldman, L. R., Greenhalgh, T., Gurdasani, D., Hamdy, A., Hanage, W. P., Hodcroft, E. B., Hyde, Z., Kellam, P., Kelly-Irving, M., Krammer, F., Lipsitch, M., et al. (2020). Scientific consensus on the COVID-19 pandemic: We need to act now. *The Lancet, 396*(10260), e71–e72. https://doi.org/10.1016/S0140-6736(20)32153-X

Anderberg, J. (2022). *The herd: How Sweden chose its own path through the worst pandemic in 100 years* (A. E. Olsson, Trans.). Scribe US.

Ankel, S. (2020, February 5). A construction expert broke down how China built an emergency hospital to treat Wuhan coronavirus patients in just 10 days. *Business Insider*.

O. Erdem, *The Socioeconomic Impact of Pandemics*,
https://doi.org/10.1007/978-3-032-24189-4

Arora, G., Joshi, J., Mandal, R. S., Shrivastava, N., Virmani, R., & Sethi, T. (2021). Artificial intelligence in surveillance, diagnosis, drug discovery and vaccine development against COVID-19. *Pathogens, 10*(8), 1048. https://doi.org/10.3390/pathogens10081048

Autor, D., & Thompson, N. (2025). *Expertise*. https://doi.org/10.3386/w33941.

Ayers, J. W., Poliak, A., Dredze, M., Leas, E. C., Zhu, Z., Kelley, J. B., Faix, D. J., Goodman, A. M., Longhurst, C. A., Hogarth, M., & Smith, D. M. (2023). Comparing physician and artificial intelligence Chatbot responses to patient questions posted to a public social media forum. *JAMA Internal Medicine, 183*(6), 589. https://doi.org/10.1001/jamainternmed.2023.1838

Ball, L. M., Leigh, D., & Mishra, P. (2022). *Understanding U.S. inflation during the COVID Era* (Working Paper No. 2022/208). https://www.imf.org/en/Publications/WP/Issues/2022/10/28/Understanding-U-S-525200

Barro, R., Ursúa, J., & Weng, J. (2020). *The Coronavirus and the Great Influenza pandemic: Lessons from the "Spanish Flu" for the Coronavirus's potential effects on mortality and economic activity*. In NBER Working Paper Series. https://doi.org/10.3386/w26866.

Bendavid, E., Oh, C., Bhattacharya, J., & Ioannidis, J. P. A. (2021). Assessing mandatory stay-at-home and business closure effects on the spread of COVID-19. *European Journal of Clinical Investigation, 51*(4). https://doi.org/10.1111/eci.13484

Bolt, J., & van Zanden, J. L. (2025). Maddison-style estimates of the evolution of the world economy: A new 2023 update. *Journal of Economic Surveys, 39*(2), 631–671. https://doi.org/10.1111/joes.12618

Bradsher, K. (2024, May). Chinese scientist who shared Covid sequence protests lab closure. *The New York Times*.

Brainerd, E., & Siegler, M. V. (2003). *The economic effects of the 1918 Influenza Epidemic* (3791). https://cepr.org/publications/dp3791.

Breed, A. G. (2022, July). How an AP reporter broke the Tuskegee syphilis story. *AP*. https://apnews.com/article/tuskegee-study-experiment-syphilis-7743bd8c7d51fe0ef9a855b4bec69b1f.

Brusselaers, N., Steadson, D., Bjorklund, K., Breland, S., Stilhoff Sörensen, J., Ewing, A., Bergmann, S., & Steineck, G. (2022). Evaluation of science advice during the COVID-19 pandemic in Sweden. *Humanities and Social Sciences Communications, 9*(1), 91. https://doi.org/10.1057/s41599-022-01097-5

Brynjolfsson, E., Chandar, B., & Chen, R. (2025). Canaries in the coal mine? Six facts about the recent employment effects of artificial intelligence. *Stanford Digital Economy Working Paper*. https://digitaleconomy.stanford.edu/app/uploads/2025/11/CanariesintheCoalMine_Nov25.pdf.

Burn-Murdoch, J. (2022). Tragic fallout from the politicisation of science in the US. *Financial Times*. https://doi.org/10.1001/jamainternmed.2023.1154

Burrell, S., & Gill, G. (2005). The Liverpool cholera epidemic of 1832 and anatomical dissection—Medical mistrust and civil unrest. *Journal of the History of Medicine and Allied Sciences, 60*(4), 478–498. https://doi.org/10.1093/jhmas/jri061

Byerly, C. R. (2005). *Fever of war: The influenza epidemic in the U.S. Army during World War I.* NYU Press.

Camus, A., & Gilbert, S. (Trans.). (1991). *The plague.* Vintage International.

Cassan, G., & Van Steenvoort, M. (2021). Political regime and COVID 19 death rate: Efficient, biasing or simply different autocracies? An econometric analysis. *SSM—Population Health, 16,* 100912. https://doi.org/10.1016/j.ssmph.2021.100912

Cauchemez, S., Ferguson, N. M., Wachtel, C., Tegnell, A., Saour, G., Duncan, B., & Nicoll, A. (2009). Closure of schools during an influenza pandemic. *The Lancet Infectious Diseases, 9*(8), 473–481. https://doi.org/10.1016/S1473-3099(09)70176-8

Cervia-Hasler, C., Brüningk, S. C., Hoch, T., Fan, B., Muzio, G., Thompson, R. C., Ceglarek, L., Meledin, R., Westermann, P., Emmenegger, M., Taeschler, P., Zurbuchen, Y., Pons, M., Menges, D., Ballouz, T., Cervia-Hasler, S., Adamo, S., Merad, M., Charney, A. W., … Boyman, O. (2024). Persistent complement dysregulation with signs of thromboinflammation in active long Covid. *Science, 383*(6680). https://doi.org/10.1126/science.adg7942.

Chancel, L., Piketty, T., Saez, E., & Zucman, G. (2022). *World Inequality Report 2022.* https://wir2022.wid.world/www-site/uploads/2022/01/Summary_WorldInequalityReport2022_English.pdf.

Chen, R. C., Haynes, K., Du, S., Barron, J., & Katz, A. J. (2021). Association of cancer screening deficit in the United States with the COVID-19 pandemic. *JAMA Oncology, 7*(6), 878. https://doi.org/10.1001/jamaoncol.2021.0884

Chen, S., Igan, D., Lee, D., & Mishra, P. (2024). *Inflation and labor markets: A bottom-up view.* IMF Working Paper.

Cheng, V. C. C., Lau, S. K. P., Woo, P. C. Y., & Yuen, K. Y. (2007). Severe acute respiratory syndrome coronavirus as an agent of emerging and Reemerging infection. *Clinical Microbiology Reviews, 20*(4), 660–694. https://doi.org/10.1128/CMR.00023-07

Christakis, N. A. (2020). *Apollo's arrow: The profound and enduring impact of coronavirus on the way we live.* Little, Brown Spark.

Cohen, A. (2021, May 10). How to quit your job in the great post pandemic resignation boom. *Bloomberg.*

Congress of the United States Congressional Budget Office. (2020). *The Budget and Economic Outlook: 2020 to 2030.* https://www.cbo.gov/system/files/2020-01/56020-CBO-Outlook.pdf.

Crato, N., & Patrinos, H. A. (2025). *Improving national education systems after COVID-19: Moving forward after PIRLS 2021 and PISA 2022.* Springer.

Crosby, A. W. (2003). *America's forgotten pandemic: The influenza of 1918*. Cambridge University Press.

D'Lima, W., Lopez, L. A., & Pradhan, A. (2022). COVID-19 and housing market effects: Evidence from U.S. shutdown orders. *Real Estate Economics, 50*(2), 303–339. https://doi.org/10.1111/1540-6229.12368

Dabla-Norris, E., & Furceri, D. (2025, May 29). Debt is higher and rising faster in 80 percent of global economy.

Daniel, L. (2024, December 5). China's surveillance state is losing its grip. *Forbes*. https://www.forbes.com/sites/larsdaniel/2024/12/05/chinas-surveillance-state-is-losing-its-grip/.

Dasgupta, S. (2022). School in the time of Covid. *Monash Bioethics Review, 40*(1), 120–144. https://doi.org/10.1007/s40592-022-00161-9

Davis, D. A. (2011). The forgotten apocalypse: Katherine Anne Porter's "Pale Horse, Pale Rider," traumatic memory, and the influenza pandemic of 1918. *The Southern Literary Journal, 43*(2), 55–74. http://www.jstor.org/stable/23208856

Davis, K. C. (2018). *More deadly than war: The hidden history of the Spanish flu and the First World War*. Henry Holt and Company.

Davis, J. M. P. M., Dedon, J. L., Hoffman, M. S., Baker-White, J. M. A., Engleman, J. D., & Sunshine, J. G. (2023). Emergency powers and the pandemic: Reflecting on state legislative reforms and the future of public health response. *Journal of Emergency Management, 21*(7), 19–35. https://doi.org/10.5055/jem.0772

Delventhal, M. J., Kwon, E., & Parkhomenko, A. (2022). JUE insight: How do cities change when we work from home? *Journal of Urban Economics, 127*, 103331. https://doi.org/10.1016/j.jue.2021.103331

Demirgüç-Kunt, A., Lokshin, M., & Torre, I. (2021). The sooner, the better: The economic impact of non-pharmaceutical interventions during the early stage of the COVID-19 pandemic. *Economics of Transition and Institutional Change, 29*(4), 551–573. https://doi.org/10.1111/ecot.12284

Diamond, J. M. (2017). *Guns, germs, and steel: The fates of human societies*. Norton.

Ding, X., Shang, B., Xie, C., Xin, J., & Yu, F. (2025). Artificial intelligence in the COVID-19 pandemic: Balancing benefits and ethical challenges in China's response. *Humanities and Social Sciences Communications, 12*(1), 245. https://doi.org/10.1057/s41599-025-04564-x

Egger, D., Miguel, E., Warren, S. S., Shenoy, A., Collins, E., Karlan, D., Parkerson, D., Mobarak, A. M., Fink, G., Udry, C., Walker, M., Haushofer, J., Larreboure, M., Athey, S., Lopez-Pena, P., Benhachmi, S., Humphreys, M., Lowe, L., Meriggi, N. F., … Vernot, C. (2021). Falling living standards during the COVID-19 crisis: Quantitative evidence from nine developing countries *Science Advances, 7*(6). https://doi.org/10.1126/sciadv.abe0997.

Encyclopedia.com. (2025, May 7). *"Porter, Katherine Anne 1890–1980." https://www.encyclopedia.com/arts/culture-magazines/porter-katherine-anne-1890-1980*

Erdbrink, T. (2020, June 22). Sweden tries out a new status: Pariah state. *The New York Times*. https://www.nytimes.com/2020/06/22/world/europe/sweden-coronavirus-pariah-scandinavia.html.

Erdem, O. (2020a). *After the crash*. Springer International Publishing. https://doi.org/10.1007/978-3-030-43343-7.

Erdem, O. (2020b). Freedom and stock market performance during Covid-19 outbreak. *Finance Research Letters, 36*, 101671. https://doi.org/10.1016/J.FRL.2020.101671

Erdem, O., & Gider, Z. (2025). The pandemic puzzle: The causal impact of government stringency on housing prices. *International Journal of Housing Markets and Analysis*. https://doi.org/10.1108/IJHMA-01-2025-0015

Erdem, O., Hassett, K., & Egriboyun, F. (2025). Hallucination in AI-generated financial literature reviews: Evaluating bibliographic accuracy. *International Journal of Data Science and Analytics*. https://doi.org/10.1007/s41060-025-00731-0

Eymeoud, J.-B., Petrosky-Nadeau, N., Santaeulàlia-Llopis, R., & Wasmer, E. (2021). *Contrasting U.S. and European job markets during COVID-19*. https://www.frbsf.org/wp-content/uploads/el2021-05.pdf.

Fairlie, R., Fossen, F. M., Johnsen, R., & Droboniku, G. (2023). Were small businesses more likely to permanently close in the pandemic? *Small Business Economics, 60*(4), 1613–1629. https://doi.org/10.1007/s11187-022-00662-1

Ferguson, N. M., Laydon, D., Nedjati-Gilani, G., Imai, N., Ainslie, K., Baguelin, M., Bhatia, S., Boonyasiri, A., Cucunubá, Z., Cuomo-Dannenburg, G., Dighe, A., Dorigatti, I., Fu, H., Gaythorpe, K., Green, W., Hamlet, A., Hinsley, W., Okell, L. C., Van Elsland, S., … Ghani, A. C. (2020). *Report 9: Impact of non-pharmaceutical interventions (NPIs) to reduce COVID-19 mortality and healthcare demand*. https://doi.org/10.25561/77482.

Foster, T. B., Fernandez, L., Porter, S. R., & Pharris-Ciurej, N. (2024). Racial and ethnic disparities in excess all-cause mortality in the first year of the COVID-19 pandemic. *Demography, 61*(1), 59–85. https://doi.org/10.1215/00703370-11133943

Gadarian, S. K., Goodman, S. W., & Pepinsky, T. B. (2021). Partisanship, health behavior, and policy attitudes in the early stages of the COVID-19 pandemic. *PLoS One, 16*(4), e0249596. https://doi.org/10.1371/journal.pone.0249596

Giesecke, J. (2020). The invisible pandemic. *The Lancet, 395*(10238), e98. https://doi.org/10.1016/S0140-6736(20)31035-7

Givner, J. (1979). Katherine Anne Porter, Journalist. *Southwest Review*.

Glass, R. J., Glass, L. M., Beyeler, W. E., & Min, H. J. (2006). Targeted social distancing designs for pandemic influenza. *Emerging Infectious Diseases, 12*(11), 1671–1681. https://doi.org/10.3201/eid1211.060255

Glassman, A., Kenny, C., & Yang, G. (2022). COVID-19 vaccine development and rollout in historical perspective. Center for Global Development. Working Paper 607.

Global Economic Prospects, June 2025. (2025). International Bank for Reconstruction and Development/The World Bank. https://www.worldbank.org/en/publication/global-economic-prospects.

Global Preparedness Monitoring Board. (2019). *A world at risk: Annual Report on Global Preparedness for Health Emergencies.* https://www.gpmb.org/docs/librariesprovider17/default-document-library/annual-reports/gpmb-2019-annualreport-en.pdf?sfvrsn=d1c9143c_30.

Global Preparedness Monitoring Board. (2020). *A world in disorder: Global Preparedness Monitoring Board Annual Report 2020. World Health Organization.*

Goldhaber, D., Kane, T. J., McEachin, A., Morton, E., Patterson, T., & Staiger, D. O. (2023). The educational consequences of remote and hybrid instruction during the pandemic. *American Economic Review: Insights, 5*(3), 377–392. https://doi.org/10.1257/aeri.20220180

Gottlieb, C., Grobovšek, J., Poschke, M., & Saltiel, F. (2022). Lockdown accounting. *The B.E. Journal of Macroeconomics, 22*(1), 197–210. https://doi.org/10.1515/bejm-2020-0251

Green, T. (2021). *The Covid consensus: The new politics of global inequality.* Hurst.

Gupta, A., Mittal, V., Peeters, J., & Van Nieuwerburgh, S. (2022). Flattening the curve: Pandemic-induced revaluation of urban real estate. *Journal of Financial Economics, 146*(2), 594–636. https://doi.org/10.1016/j.jfineco.2021.10.008

Ha, H., Knox, C., & Janenova, S. (2024). Authoritarian and democratic states: The COVID-19 pandemic and the efficacy of public health outcomes. *Journal of Public Policy, 44*(4), 767–784. https://doi.org/10.1017/S0143814X24000163

Haerpfer, C., Inglehart, R., Moreno, A., Welzel, C., Kizilova, K., Diez-Medrano J., Lagos, M., Norris, P., Ponarin, E., & Puranen, B., Eds. (2022). *World values survey: Round seven—Country-pooled Datafile Version 4.0.* https://doi.org/10.14281/18241.18.

Hale, T., Angrist, N., Goldszmidt, R., Kira, B., Petherick, A., Phillips, T., Webster, S., Cameron-Blake, E., Hallas, L., Majumdar, S., & Tatlow, H. (2021). A global panel database of pandemic policies (Oxford COVID-19 Government Response Tracker). *Nature Human Behaviour, 5*(4), 529–538. https://doi.org/10.1038/s41562-021-01079-8

Harper, K. (2017). *The fate of Rome: Climate, disease, and the end of an empire* (ebook). Princeton University Press.

Hartnett, K. P., Kite-Powell, A., DeVies, J., Coletta, M. A., Boehmer, T. K., Adjemian, J., & Gundlapalli, A. V. (2020). *Impact of the COVID-19 pandemic on emergency department visits—United States, January 1, 2019–May 30, 2020.* https://www.cdc.gov/mmwr/volumes/69/wr/mm6923e1.htm?s_cid=mm6923e1_w.

Hartney, M. T., & Finger, L. K. (2022). Politics, markets, and pandemics: Public education's response to COVID-19. *Perspectives on Politics, 20*(2), 457–473. https://doi.org/10.1017/S1537592721000955

Hatchett, R. J., Mecher, C. E., & Lipsitch, M. (2007). Public health interventions and epidemic intensity during the 1918 influenza pandemic. *Proceedings of the National Academy of Sciences, 104*(18), 7582–7587. https://doi.org/10.1073/pnas.0610941104

Hauser, C. (2020, December 10). The mask slackers of 1918. *The New York Times.*

Hendrycks, D., Mazeika, M., & Woodside, T. (2023). An overview of catastrophic AI risks. https://doi.org/10.48550/arXiv.2306.12001

Henley, J. (2020, March 23). Swedish PM warned over "Russian roulette-style" Covid-19 strategy. *The Guardian.* https://www.theguardian.com/world/2020/mar/23/swedish-pm-warned-russian-roulette-covid-19-strategy-herd-immunity.

Hill, L., & Artiga, S. (2022). *COVID-19 cases and deaths by race/ethnicity: Current data and changes over time.* https://www.kff.org/racial-equity-and-health-policy/issue-brief/covid-19-cases-and-deaths-by-race-ethnicity-current-data-and-changes-over-time/?utm_.

Holmes, E. (2020). *Novel 2019 coronavirus genome.* Virological.org. Available at: https://virological.org/t/novel-2019-coronavirus-genome/319

Hook, L. (2020, October 29). The next pandemic: Where is it coming from and how do we stop it? *Financial Times.* https://www.ft.com/content/2a80e4a2-7fb9-4e2c-9769-bc0d98382a5c.

Hsiang, S., Allen, D., Annan-Phan, S., Bell, K., Bolliger, I., Chong, T., Druckenmiller, H., Huang, L. Y., Hultgren, A., Krasovich, E., Lau, P., Lee, J., Rolf, E., Tseng, J., & Wu, T. (2020). The effect of large-scale anti-contagion policies on the COVID-19 pandemic. *Nature, 584*(7820), 262–267. https://doi.org/10.1038/s41586-020-2404-8

Hsu, A. (2021, June 24). As the pandemic recedes, millions of workers are saying "I Quit." *NPR.* https://www.npr.org/2021/06/24/1007914455/as-the-pandemic-recedes-millions-of-workers-are-saying-i-quit.

Hussain, T., Wang, D., & Li, B. (2024). The influence of the COVID-19 pandemic on the adoption and impact of AI ChatGPT: Challenges, applications, and ethical considerations. *Acta Psychologica, 246*, 104264. https://doi.org/10.1016/j.actpsy.2024.104264

Imtiaz, S., Nafeh, F., Russell, C., Ali, F., Elton-Marshall, T., & Rehm, J. (2021). The impact of the novel coronavirus disease (COVID-19) pandemic on drug overdose-related deaths in the United States and Canada: A systematic review of observational studies and analysis of public health surveillance data. *Substance Abuse Treatment, Prevention, and Policy, 16*(1), 87. https://doi.org/10.1186/s13011-021-00423-5

Irwin, R. E. (2020). Misinformation and de-contextualization: International media reporting on Sweden and COVID-19. *Globalization and Health, 16*(1), 62. https://doi.org/10.1186/s12992-020-00588-x

Jefferson, T., Dooley, L., Ferroni, E., Al-Ansary, L. A., van Driel, M. L., Bawazeer, G. A., Jones, M. A., Hoffmann, T. C., Clark, J., Beller, E. M., Glasziou, P. P., & Conly, J. M. (2023). Physical interventions to interrupt or reduce the spread of respiratory viruses. *Cochrane Database of Systematic Reviews, 2023*(4). https://doi.org/10.1002/14651858.CD006207.pub6

Jennings, W., Valgarðsson, V., McKay, L., Stoker, G., Mello, E., & Baniamin, H. M. (2023). Trust and vaccine hesitancy during the COVID-19 pandemic: A cross-national analysis. *Vaccine, X*(14), 100299. https://doi.org/10.1016/j.jvacx.2023.100299

Jin, C., Chen, W., Cao, Y., Xu, Z., Tan, Z., Zhang, X., Deng, L., Zheng, C., Zhou, J., Shi, H., & Feng, J. (2020). Development and evaluation of an artificial intelligence system for COVID-19 diagnosis. *Nature Communications, 11*(1), 5088. https://doi.org/10.1038/s41467-020-18685-1

Johnson, N. P. A. S., & Mueller, J. (2002). Updating the accounts: Global mortality of the 1918–1920 "Spanish" influenza pandemic. *Bulletin of the History of Medicine, 76*(1), 105–115. https://doi.org/10.1353/bhm.2002.0022

Jones, K. E., Patel, N. G., Levy, M. A., Storeygard, A., Balk, D., Gittleman, J. L., & Daszak, P. (2008). Global trends in emerging infectious diseases. *Nature, 451*(7181), 990–993. https://doi.org/10.1038/nature06536

Kahl, C., & Wright, T. (2021). *Aftershocks: Pandemic politics and the end of the old international order.* Martin's Press.

Kamenetz, A. (2021, September 1). National survey finds severe and desperate school bus driver shortage. *NPR*. https://www.npr.org/sections/back-to-school-live-updates/2021/09/01/1032953269/national-survey-finds-severe-and-desperate-school-bus-driver-shortage.

Kane, T., & Reardon, S. (2023, May 11). *Parents don't understand how far behind their kids are in school.* https://www.nytimes.com/interactive/2023/05/11/opinion/pandemic-learning-losses-steep-but-not-permanent.html.

Kapiriri, L., Kiwanuka, S., Biemba, G., Velez, C., Razavi, S. D., Abelson, J., Essue, B. M., Danis, M., Goold, S., Noorulhuda, M., Nouvet, E., Sandman, L., & Williams, I. (2022). Priority setting and equity in COVID-19 pandemic plans: A comparative analysis of 18 African countries. *Health Policy and Planning, 37*(3), 297–309. https://doi.org/10.1093/heapol/czab113

Karikó, K. (2023). *Breaking through: My life in science.* Crown.

Karikó, K., Buckstein, M., Ni, H., & Weissman, D. (2005). Suppression of RNA recognition by toll-like receptors: The impact of nucleoside modification and the evolutionary origin of RNA. *Immunity, 23*(2), 165–175. https://doi.org/10.1016/j.immuni.2005.06.008

Karlinsky, A., & Kobak, D. (2021). Tracking excess mortality across countries during the COVID-19 pandemic with the world mortality dataset. *ELife, 10*. https://doi.org/10.7554/eLife.69336

Kolata, G. (2021, April 8). *Long overlooked, Kati Kariko helped shield the world from the Coronavirus*. https://www.nytimes.com/2021/04/08/health/coronavirus-mrna-kariko.html?searchResultPosition=1.

Krizhevsky, A., Sutskever, I., & Hinton, G. E. (2012). ImageNet classification with deep convolutional neural networks. In F. Pereira, C. J. Burges, L. Bottou, & K. Q. Weinberger (Eds.), *Advances in neural information processing systems* (Vol. 25). https://doi.org/10.1145/3065386.

Kuenssberg, L. (2021, March 15). Covid: The inside story of the government's battle against the virus. *BBC*. https://www.bbc.com/news/uk-politics-56361599.

Laurens, M. B. (2020). RTS,S/AS01 vaccine (Mosquirix™): An overview. *Human Vaccines & Immunotherapeutics, 16*(3), 480–489. https://doi.org/10.1080/21645515.2019.1669415

Leung, C. M. C., Ho, M. K., Bharwani, A. A., Cogo-Moreira, H., Wang, Y., Chow, M. S. C., Fan, X., Galea, S., Leung, G. M., & Ni, M. Y. (2022). Mental disorders following COVID-19 and other epidemics: A systematic review and meta-analysis. *Translational Psychiatry, 12*(1), 205. https://doi.org/10.1038/s41398-022-01946-6

Lewis, M. (2021). *The premonition: A pandemic story*. Norton.

Li, L., Taeihagh, A., & Tan, S. Y. (2023). A scoping review of the impacts of COVID-19 physical distancing measures on vulnerable population groups. *Nature Communications, 14*(1), 599. https://doi.org/10.1038/s41467-023-36267-9

Lønborg, J. H., Viveros, M., Aguilar, R. A. C., Lakner, C., Ibarra, G. L., Nguyen, M. C., & Baah, S. K. T. (2025, June 5). *June 2025 global poverty update from the World Bank: 2021 PPPs and new country-data*. Poverty and Inequality Platform. https://blogs.worldbank.org/en/opendata/june-2025-global-poverty-update-from-the-world-bank%2D%2D2021-ppps-a.

Lovgren, S. (2005, July 6). "Guns, germs and steel": Jared Diamond Interview. https://www.nationalgeographic.com/science/article/news-guns-germs-steel-jared-diamond-interview

Lynch, E. A. (1998). The flu of 1918. Pennsylvania Gazette. https://thepenngazette.com/the-flu-of-1918/.

Lyu, W., & Wehby, G. L. (2020). Community use of face masks and COVID-19: Evidence from a natural experiment of state mandates in the US. *Health Affairs, 39*(8), 1419–1425. https://doi.org/10.1377/hlthaff.2020.00818

Macedo, S., & Lee, F. E. (2025). *In Covid's wake: How our politics failed us.* Princeton University Press.

Mack, A., & Martínez-García, E. (2011). *A cross-country quarterly database of real house prices: A methodological note.* https://doi.org/10.24149/gwp99

Mallin, A. (2023, February 28). "Potential lab incident": FBI director Wray speaks publicly for 1st time on COVID-19 origin. *ABC News.* https://abcnews.go.com/Politics/potential-lab-incident-fbi-director-wray-speaks-publicly/story?id=97535563.

Mamelund, S.-E. (2006). A socially neutral disease? Individual social class, household wealth and mortality from Spanish influenza in two socially contrasting parishes in Kristiania 1918–19. *Social Science & Medicine, 62*(4), 923–940. https://doi.org/10.1016/j.socscimed.2005.06.051

Marani, M., Katul, G. G., Pan, W. K., & Parolari, A. J. (2021). Intensity and frequency of extreme novel epidemics. *Proceedings of the National Academy of Sciences, 118*(35). https://doi.org/10.1073/pnas.2105482118

Maranto, R., Queiroz e Melo, R., & Glenn, C. (2023). COVID-19 and schooling in the U.S.: Disruption, continuity, quality, and equity. In *COVID-19 and schools* (pp. 6–12). Routledge. https://doi.org/10.4324/9781003426158-2

Markel, H., Lipman, H. B., Navarro, J. A., Sloan, A., Michalsen, J. R., Stern, A. M., & Cetron, M. S. (2007). Nonpharmaceutical interventions implemented by US cities during the 1918–1919 influenza pandemic. *JAMA, 298*(6), 644. https://doi.org/10.1001/jama.298.6.644

Marshall, D. T., Pressley, T., & Patrinos, H. A. (2024). *Lessons of the pandemic: Disruption, innovation, and what schools need to move forward.* The Guilford Press.

Martínez, J. (2017). Political consequences of the plague of Athens. *Graeco-Latina Brunensia, 1*, 135–146. https://doi.org/10.5817/GLB2017-1-12

Mathieu, E., Ritchie, H., Rodés-Guirao, L., Appel, C., Giattino, C., Ortiz-Ospina Esteban, Hasell, J., Macdonald, B., Beltekian, D., & Roser, M. (2020). *Coronavirus pandemic (COVID-19).* https://ourworldindata.org/coronavirus.

Mayor, A. (2023). Talos, Pandora, and the Trojan horse as products of technology in ancient literature and art. *E-Phaïstos, XI*(1). https://doi.org/10.4000/ephaistos.10885

McCarthy, J., Minsky, M. L., Rochester, N., & Shannon, C. E. (1955, August 31). *A proposal for The Dartmouth Summer Research Project on Artificial Intelligence.* http://jmc.stanford.edu/articles/dartmouth/dartmouth.pdf.

McGowan, V. J., & Bambra, C. (2022). COVID-19 mortality and deprivation: Pandemic, syndemic, and endemic health inequalities. *The Lancet Public Health, 7*(11), e966–e975. https://doi.org/10.1016/S2468-2667(22)00223-7

McNutt, M., Anderson, J. L., & Dzau, V. J. (2021, June 15). *Let scientific evidence determine origin of SARS-CoV-2, urge presidents of the National Academies.* Statement.

Mendoza Cardozo, O. I., Pérez Bedoya, J. P., Ruiz Galvis, L. M., Pérez Aguirre, C. A., Rodríguez Rey, B. A., Barengo, N. C., Cardona Jiménez, J., & Díaz Valencia, P. A. (2023). Socioeconomic disparities associated with mortality in patients hospitalized for COVID-19 in Colombia. *Frontiers in Public Health, 11*. https://doi.org/10.3389/fpubh.2023.1139379

Miller, J., Tureci, O., & Sahin, U. (2022). *The vaccine: Inside the race to conquer the Covid-19 pandemic*. St. Martin's Press.

Mills, C. K., & Battisto, J. (2020). *Double Jeopardy: Covid-19's concentrated health and wealth effects in Black communities*. https://www.newyorkfed.org/medialibrary/media/smallbusiness/DoubleJeopardy_COVID19andBlackOwnedBusinesses.

Moritsugu, K., & Wang, Y. (2020, January 23). China confirms 1st death outside epicenter of viral outbreak. *AP*.

Mukherjee, S., Kshirsagar, M., Becker, N., Xu, Y., Weeks, W. B., Patel, S., Ferres, J. L., & Jackson, M. L. (2022). Identifying long-term effects of SARS-CoV-2 and their association with social determinants of health in a cohort of over one million COVID-19 survivors. *BMC Public Health, 22*(1), 2394. https://doi.org/10.1186/s12889-022-14806-1

Mukherji, R. (2020). Covid vs. democracy: India's illiberal remedy. *Journal of Democracy, 31*(4), 91–105. https://doi.org/10.1353/jod.2020.0058

Mulet, J. M. (2019, November 23). El obispo de Zamora que desafió a la gripe en nombre de la fe (*The Bishop of Zamora who defied the flu in the name of faith). El Pais*. https://elpais.com/elpais/2019/11/18/eps/1574101346_748744.html

Myhrvold, N. (2013). Strategic terrorism: A call to action. *SSRN Electronic Journal*. https://doi.org/10.2139/ssrn.2290382

Narayanan, A., & Kapoor, S. (2024). *AI snake oil: What artificial intelligence can do, what it can't, and how to tell the difference*. Princeton University Press.

National Intelligence Council. (2004). *Mapping the global future: 3 Report of the National Intelligence Council's 2020 Project*. https://www.dni.gov/files/documents/Global%20Trends_Mapping%20the%20Global%20Future%202020%20Project.pdf.

National Research Council. (2016). *The neglected dimension of global security*. National Academies Press. https://doi.org/10.17226/21891

Newey, S., & Nuki, P. (2020, December 2). *"Redemption": How a scientist's unwavering belief in mRNA gave the world a Covid-19 vaccine*. https://www.telegraph.co.uk/global-health/science-and-disease/redemption-one-scientists-unwavering-belief-mrna-gave-world/.

Nivette, A. E., Zahnow, R., Aguilar, R., Ahven, A., Amram, S., Ariel, B., Burbano, M. J. A., Astolfi, R., Baier, D., Bark, H. M., Beijers, J. E. H., Bergman, M., Breetzke, G., Concha-Eastman, I. A., Curtis-Ham, S., Davenport, R., Díaz, C., Fleitas, D., Gerell, M., et al. (2021). A global analysis of the impact of

COVID-19 stay-at-home restrictions on crime. *Nature Human Behaviour, 5*(7), 868–877. https://doi.org/10.1038/s41562-021-01139-z

Nori, H., Daswani, M., & Kelly, C. (2025). Sequential diagnosis with language models. *Arxiv.* https://doi.org/10.48550/arXiv.2506.22405

Noy, S., & Zhang, W. (2023). Experimental evidence on the productivity effects of generative artificial intelligence. *Science, 381*(6654), 187–192. https://doi.org/10.1126/science.adh2586

Nuclear Threat Initiative. (2019). *Global Health Security Index: Building collective action and accountability.* http://www.jstor.org/stable/resrep44061.

OECD. (2023). *PISA 2022 results (Volume I).* OECD. https://doi.org/10.1787/53f23881-en.

Office for National Statistics. (2021, February 12). *GDP first quarterly estimate, UK: October to December 2020.* https://www.ons.gov.uk/economy/grossdomesticproductgdp/bulletins/gdpfirstquarterlyestimateuk/octobertodecember2020.

Ozdemir, D. Y., Ayvaci, M., & Zentner, A. (2024). What people think of machines as doctors: Unveiling the value of Gen-AI for e-health. *SSRN Electronic Journal.* https://doi.org/10.2139/ssrn.4765222

Pamuk, Ş., & Shatzmiller, M. (2014). Plagues, wages, and economic change in the Islamic Middle East, 700–1500. *The Journal of Economic History, 74*(1), 196–229. https://doi.org/10.1017/S0022050714000072

Pardi, N., Hogan, M. J., Pelc, R. S., Muramatsu, H., Andersen, H., DeMaso, C. R., Dowd, K. A., Sutherland, L. L., Scearce, R. M., Parks, R., Wagner, W., Granados, A., Greenhouse, J., Walker, M., Willis, E., Yu, J.-S., McGee, C. E., Sempowski, G. D., Mui, B. L., et al. (2017). Zika virus protection by a single low-dose nucleoside-modified mRNA vaccination. *Nature, 543*(7644), 248–251. https://doi.org/10.1038/nature21428

Patrinos, H. A. (2023). The longer students were out of school, the less they learned. *Journal of School Choice, 17*(2), 161–175. https://doi.org/10.1080/15582159.2023.2210941

Pecetta, S., Tortorice, D., Scorza, F. B., Pizza, M., Dougan, G., Hatchett, R., Black, S., Bloom, D. E., & Rappuoli, R. (2022). The trillion dollar vaccine gap. *Science Translational Medicine, 14*(638). https://doi.org/10.1126/scitranslmed.abn4342

Pew Research Center. (2024). *Representative democracy remains a popular ideal, but people around the world are critical of how it's working.* https://www.pewresearch.org/global/2024/02/28/representative-democracy-remains-a-popular-ideal-but-people-around-the-world-are-critical-of-how-its-working/

Pierre, J. (2020). Nudges against pandemics: Sweden's COVID-19 containment strategy in perspective. *Policy and Society, 39*(3), 478–493. https://doi.org/10.1080/14494035.2020.1783787

Piketty, T., & Couper, K. (2021). *Time for socialism: Dispatches from a world on fire, 2016–2021.* Yale University Press.

Pizzato, M., Gerli, A. G., La Vecchia, C., & Alicandro, G. (2024). Impact of COVID-19 on total excess mortality and geographic disparities in Europe, 2020–2023: A spatio-temporal analysis. *The Lancet Regional Health—Europe, 44*, 100996. https://doi.org/10.1016/j.lanepe.2024.100996

Porter, K. A. (2008). *Pale horse, pale rider three short novels.* The Library of America.

Prakash, N., Srivastava, B., Singh, S., Sharma, S., & Jain, S. (2022). Effectiveness of social distancing interventions in containing COVID-19 incidence: International evidence using Kalman filter. *Economics & Human Biology, 44*, 101091. https://doi.org/10.1016/j.ehb.2021.101091

Prommas, P., Lwin, K. S., Chen, Y. C., Hyakutake, M., Ghaznavi, C., Sakamoto, H., Miyata, H., & Nomura, S. (2023). The impact of social isolation from COVID-19-related public health measures on cognitive function and mental health among older adults: A systematic review and meta-analysis. *Ageing Research Reviews, 85*, 101839. https://doi.org/10.1016/j.arr.2022.101839

Psacharopoulos, G., Collis, V., Patrinos, H. A., & Vegas, E. (2021). The COVID-19 cost of school closures in earnings and income across the world. *Comparative Education Review, 65*(2), 271–287. https://doi.org/10.1086/713540

Reinhart, C. M., & Rogoff, K. S. (2014). Recovery from financial crises: Evidence from 100 episodes. *American Economic Review, 104*(5), 50–55. https://doi.org/10.1257/aer.104.5.50

Sahel, J.-A., Boulanger-Scemama, E., Pagot, C., Arleo, A., Galluppi, F., Martel, J. N., Esposti, S. D., Delaux, A., de Saint Aubert, J.-B., de Montleau, C., Gutman, E., Audo, I., Duebel, J., Picaud, S., Dalkara, D., Blouin, L., Taiel, M., & Roska, B. (2021). Partial recovery of visual function in a blind patient after optogenetic therapy. *Nature Medicine, 27*(7), 1223–1229. https://doi.org/10.1038/s41591-021-01351-4

Sander, B., Nizam, A., Garrison, L. P., Postma, M. J., Halloran, M. E., & Longini, I. M. (2009). Economic evaluation of influenza pandemic mitigation strategies in the United States using a stochastic microsimulation transmission model. *Value in Health, 12*(2), 226–233. https://doi.org/10.1111/J.1524-4733.2008.00437.X

Sandford, A. (2020, February 4). Coronavirus: Half of humanity now on lockdown as 90 countries call for confinement. *Euronews.* https://www.euronews.com/2020/04/02/coronavirus-in-europe-spain-s-death-toll-hits-10-000-after-record-950-new-deaths-in-24-hou.

Sarris, P. (2022). Viewpoint new approaches to the 'Plague of Justinian'. *Past & Present, 254*(1), 315–346. https://doi.org/10.1093/pastj/gtab024

Shannon, C. E. (1948). A mathematical theory of communication. *Bell System Technical Journal, 27*(3), 379–423. https://doi.org/10.1002/j.1538-7305.1948.tb01338.x

Sherif, M., & Sherif, C. W. (1953). *Groups in harmony and tension*. Harper &Brothers Publishers.

Shukla, P., Lee, M., Whitman, S. A., & Pine, K. H. (2022). Delay of routine health care during the COVID-19 pandemic: A theoretical model of individuals' risk assessment and decision making. *Social Science & Medicine, 307*, 115164. https://doi.org/10.1016/j.socscimed.2022.115164

Sirin, J. B. (2021). *A case study examining the provincial disparities in the distribution of Covid-19 vaccines in Turkey*. Student Paper. STVK12 20211 Lund University, Department of Political Science.

Snowden, F. (2019). *Epidemics and society: From the Black death to the present*. Yale University Press.

Sorci, G., Faivre, B., & Morand, S. (2020). Explaining among-country variation in COVID-19 case fatality rate. *Scientific Reports, 10*(1), 18909. https://doi.org/10.1038/s41598-020-75848-2

Sparks, G., Kirzinger, A., Kearney, A., Valdes, I., & Hamel, L. (2023). *KFF COVID-19 vaccine monitor November 2023: With COVID concerns lagging, most people have not gotten latest vaccine and half say they are not taking precautions this holiday season*. https://www.kff.org/coronavirus-covid-19/poll-finding/vaccine-monitor-november-2023-with-covid-concerns-lagging-most-people-have-not-gotten-latest-vaccine/.

Spinney, L. (2017). *Pale rider: The Spanish flu of 1918 and how it changed the world*. PublicAffairs Hachette Book Group.

Suleyman, M., & Bhaskar, M. (2023). *The coming wave: Technology, power, and the twenty-first century's greatest dilemma*. Crown.

Sullivan, P. (2020, December 18). *Stuck at home, people are splurging on wine and spirits*. The New York Times.

Sun, L. H. (2018, February 1). CDC to cut by 80 percent efforts to prevent global disease outbreak. *Washington Post*. https://www.washingtonpost.com/news/to-your-health/wp/2018/02/01/cdc-to-cut-by-80-percent-efforts-to-prevent-global-disease-outbreak/.

Tai, D. B. G., Sia, I. G., Doubeni, C. A., & Wieland, M. L. (2022). Disproportionate impact of COVID-19 on racial and ethnic minority groups in the United States: A 2021 update. *Journal of Racial and Ethnic Health Disparities, 9*(6), 2334–2339. https://doi.org/10.1007/s40615-021-01170-w

Taubenberger, J. K., & Morens, D. M. (2006). 1918 influenza: The mother of all pandemics. *Emerging Infectious Diseases, 12*(1), 15–22. https://doi.org/10.3201/eid1201.050979

The Economist. (2022, July 13). *Which covid-19 vaccine saved the most lives in 2021?* https://www.economist.com/graphic-detail/2022/07/13/which-covid-19-vaccine-saved-the-most-lives-in-2021?utm_content=ed-picks-article-link-1&etear=nl_special_1&utm_campaign=a.coronavirus-special-edition&utm_medium=email.internal-newsletter.np&utm_source=salesforce-marketing-cloud&utm_term=7/16/2022&utm_id=1237694.

The Guardian Staff. (2020, March 23). How coronavirus advice from Boris Johnson has changed. *The Guardian*. https://www.theguardian.com/world/2020/mar/23/how-coronavirus-advice-from-boris-johnson-has-changed.

Tooze, A. (2024, March 31). Vaccine investment is a no-brainer—So why aren't we doing it? *Financial Times*. https://www.ft.com/content/ffded995-6bed-4961-bb2f-d1262ef1b0e3?utm_source=substack&utm_medium=email.

Troesken, W. (2015). *The pox of liberty: How the constitution left Americans rich, free, and prone to infection*. The University of Chicago Press.

Turing, A. M. (1950). I.—Computing machinery and intelligence. *Mind, LIX*(236), 433–460. https://doi.org/10.1093/mind/LIX.236.433

U.S. Department of Education. (2025a). *The National Assessment of Educational Progress (NAEP) Mathematics Assessment 2024*. https://www.nationsreportcard.gov/reports/mathematics/2024/g12/.

U.S. Department of Education. (2025b). *The Nation's Report Card: 2024 reading assessment, grade 12*. https://www.nationsreportcard.gov/reports/reading/2024/g12/

U.S. Department of Education. (2025c). *The Nation's Report Card: 2024 science assessment, grade 8*. https://www.nationsreportcard.gov/reports/science/2024/.

U.S. Department of Veterans Affairs. (2022). *History of Veterans Day*. https://department.va.gov/veterans-day/history-of-veterans-day/?redirect=1#:~:text=87a)%20approved%20May%2013%2C%201938,World%20War%20II%20had%20required.

U.S. Government Accountability Office. (2023). *COVID-19 relief: Funding and spending as of Jan. 31, 2023*. https://www.gao.gov/products/gao-23-106647

United Nations Development Programme (UNDP), Global Dashboard for Vaccine Equity. (n.d.). Retrieved March 31, 2024, from https://data.undp.org/insights/vaccine-equity

Vlach, M. (2020). The Antonine Plague and impact possibilities during the Marcomannic wars. In *Marcomannic Wars and Antonine Plague: Selected essays on two disasters that shook the Roman world*. Czech Academy of Sciences, Institute of Archaeology.

Vosoughi, S., Roy, D., & Aral, S. (2018). The spread of true and false news online. *Science, 359*(6380), 1146–1151. https://doi.org/10.1126/science.aap9559

Voytko-Best, L. (2020, May 27). Coronavirus layoffs: Boeing layoffs 6,770 workers amid pandemic. *Forbes*.

Wallace, J., Goldsmith-Pinkham, P., & Schwartz, J. L. (2023). Excess death rates for republican and democratic registered voters in Florida and Ohio during the COVID-19 pandemic. *JAMA Internal Medicine, 183*(9), 916. https://doi.org/10.1001/jamainternmed.2023.1154

Watson, O. J., Barnsley, G., Toor, J., Hogan, A. B., Winskill, P., & Ghani, A. C. (2022). Global impact of the first year of COVID-19 vaccination: A mathematical modelling study. *The Lancet Infectious Diseases*. https://doi.org/10.1016/S1473-3099(22)00320-6

Weiser, B., & Schweber, N. (2023, June 8). The ChatGPT lawyer explains himself. *The New York Times*.

Weizenbaum, J. (1966). ELIZA—A computer program for the study of natural language communication between man and machine. *Communications of the ACM, 9*(1), 36–45. https://doi.org/10.1145/365153.365168

White, A. M., Castle, I.-J. P., Powell, P. A., Hingson, R. W., & Koob, G. F. (2022). Alcohol-related deaths during the COVID-19 pandemic. *JAMA, 327*(17), 1704. https://doi.org/10.1001/jama.2022.4308

Wong, A., Li, X., Lau, S., & Woo, P. (2019). Global epidemiology of bat coronaviruses. *Viruses, 11*(2), 174. https://doi.org/10.3390/v11020174

Woo, J. (2023). Financial crises and inequality: New evidence from a panel of 17 advanced economies. *The Journal of Economic Asymmetries, 28*, e00323. https://doi.org/10.1016/j.jeca.2023.e00323

World Health Organization. (2020, June 29). *Listings of WHO's response to COVID-19*. https://www.who.int/news/item/29-06-2020-covidtimeline.

World Health Organization (WHO). (2007). *The World Health Report 2007: A safer future*.

Yong, E. (2018, July). The next plague is coming. Is America ready? *The Atlantic*. https://www.theatlantic.com/magazine/archive/2018/07/when-the-next-plague-hits/561734/.

Yuko, E. (2021, March 11). How World War I's legacy eclipsed the 1918 pandemic. *History*. https://www.history.com/news/world-war-i-1918-pandemic-memorials.

Zewde, N., & Crystal, S. (2022). Impact of the 2008 recession on wealth-adjusted income and inequality for U.S. cohorts. *The Journals of Gerontology: Series B, 77*(4), 780–789. https://doi.org/10.1093/geronb/gbab141

Zizek, S. (2020). *Pandemic!: Covid-19 shakes the world*. Polity Press.

Zweig, D. (2025). *An abundance of caution: American schools, the virus, and a story of bad decisions*. The MIT Press.

Index[1]

[1] Note: Page numbers followed by 'n' refer to notes.

O. Erdem, *The Socioeconomic Impact of Pandemics*,
https://doi.org/10.1007/978-3-032-24189-4

The manufacturer's authorised representative in the EU is Springer Nature Customer Service Centre GmbH, Europaplatz 3, 69115 Heidelberg, Germany. If you have any concerns regarding our products, please contact ProductSafety@springernature.com

Printed and bound by CPI Group (UK) Ltd, Croydon, CR0 4YY
21/09/2026
02219963-0002